Keith Pepperell

Photographs III

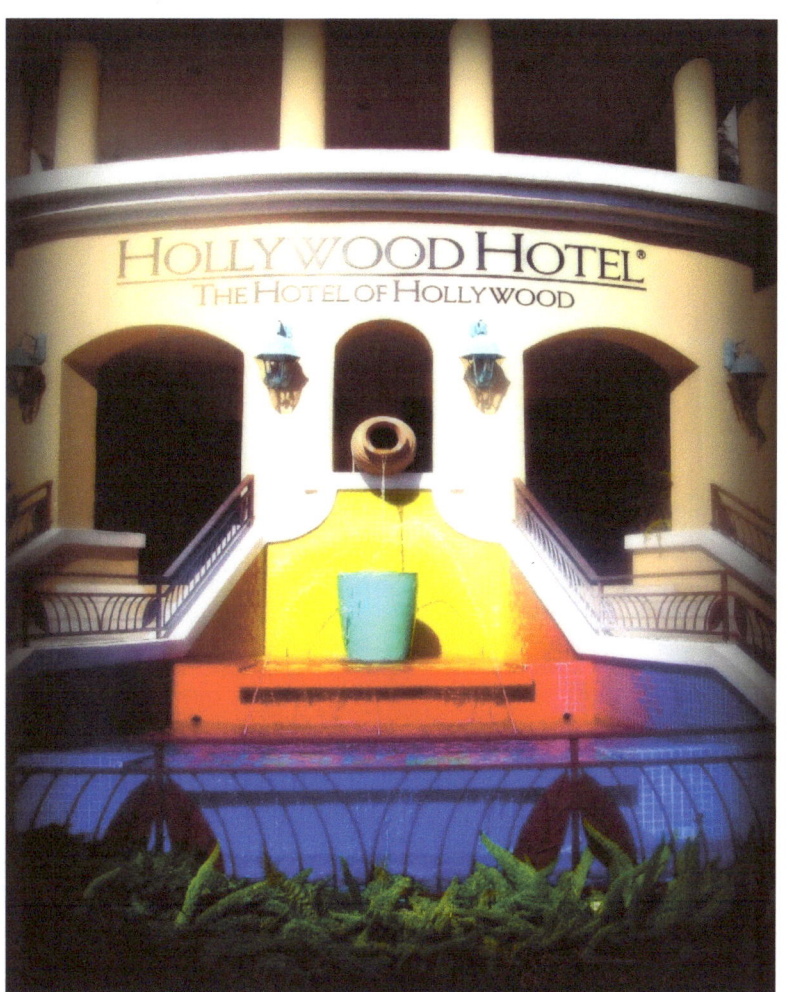

Keith Pepperell

DEDICATION

To my spawn Jack, Lydia, and Alex all of whom have taken
a snap or two

ACKNOWLEDGMENTS

Lady Joan Pepperell

Sir Francis Pepperell

Sir Arthur MacDonald (Don) Fowler

Lady Audrey Fowler

All of whom were a dab hand with a camera

THE PHOTOGRAPHS

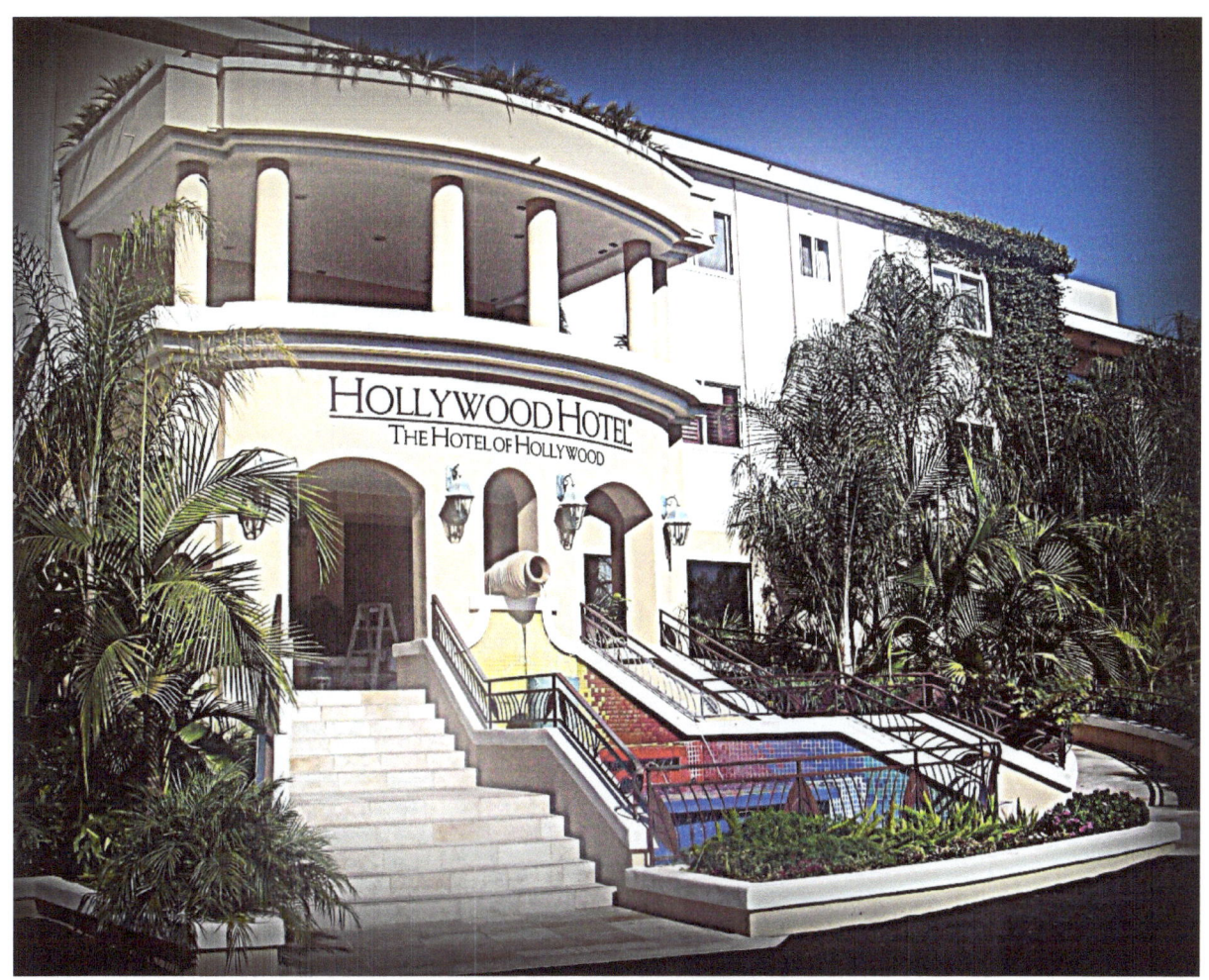

Hollywood Hotel

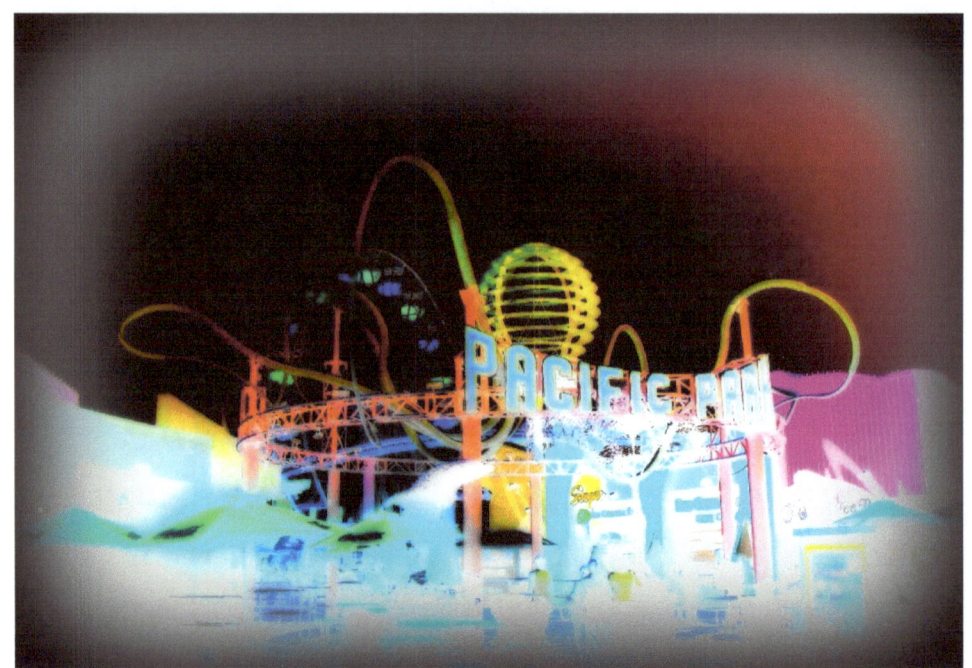

Pacific Park

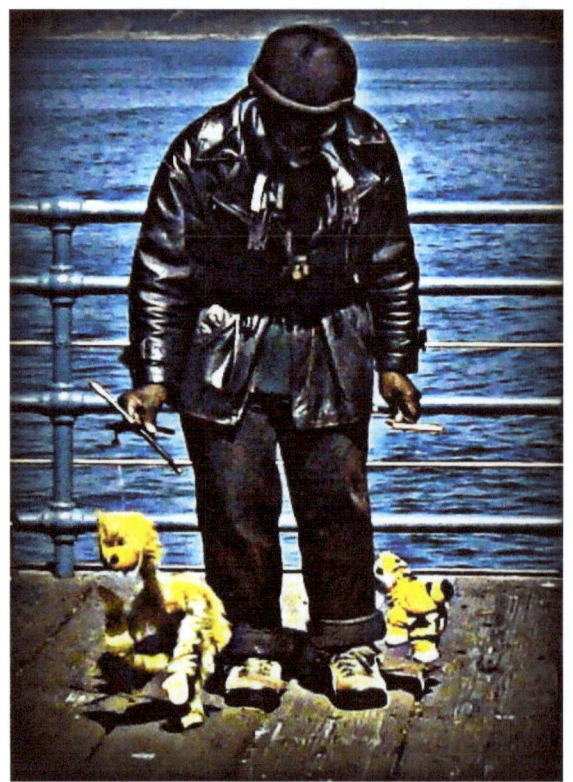

Pier Puppeteer

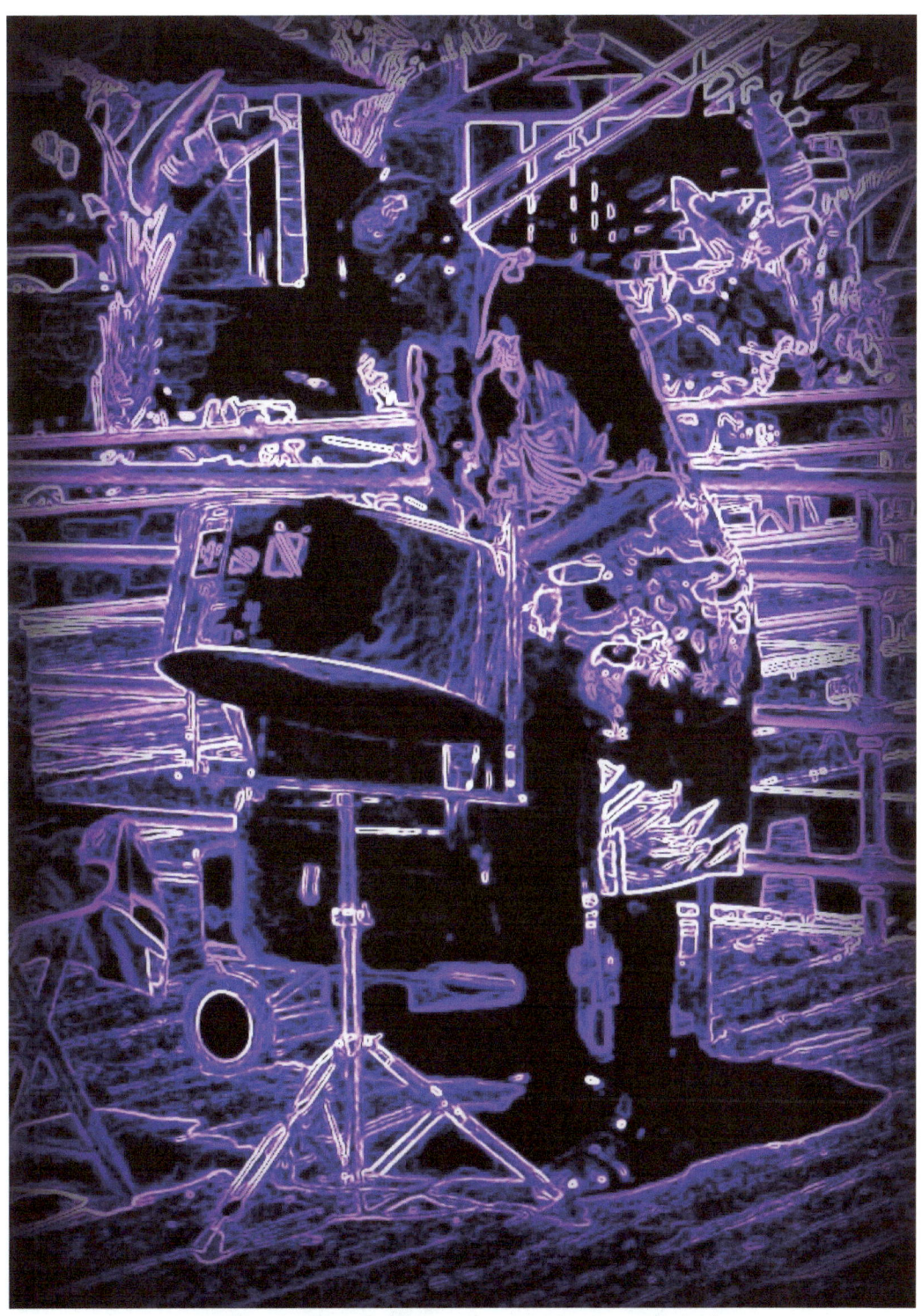

Steel Bandsman, Santa Monica

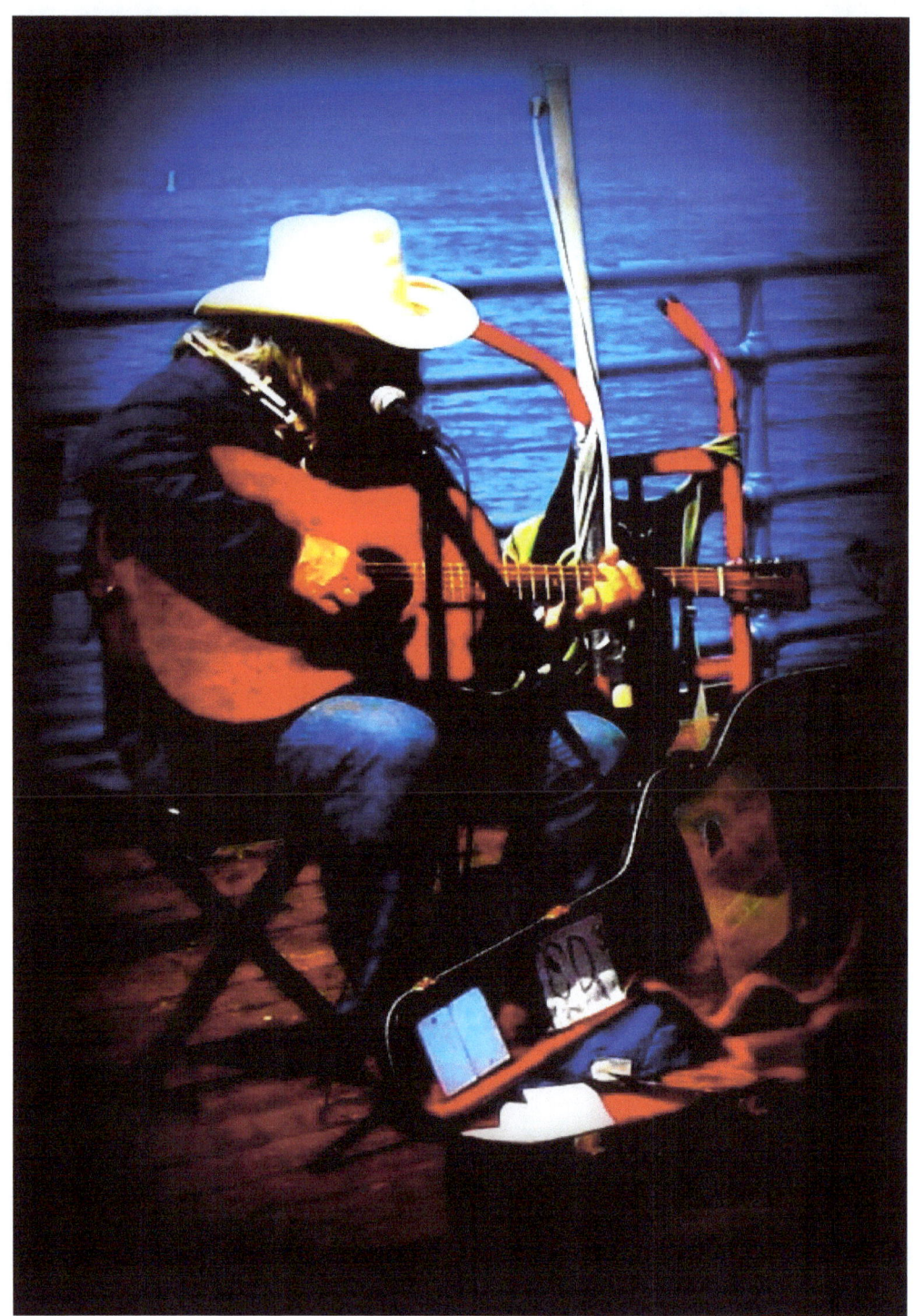

Pier Musician, Santa Monica

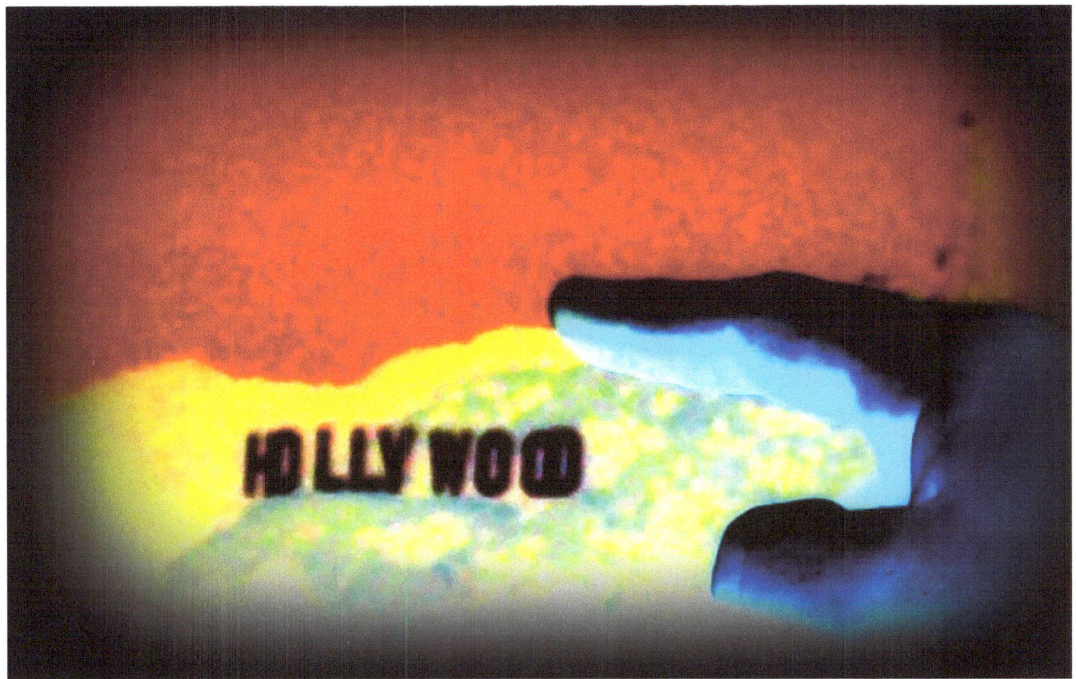

Where Dreams are Shattered

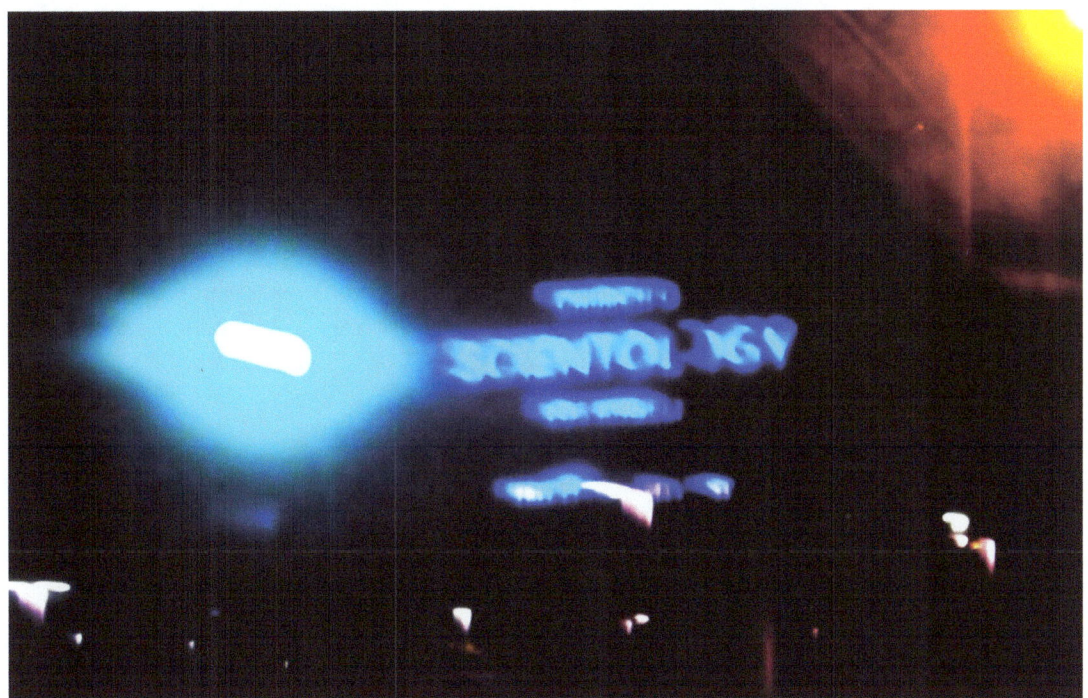

Da Do Ron Ron

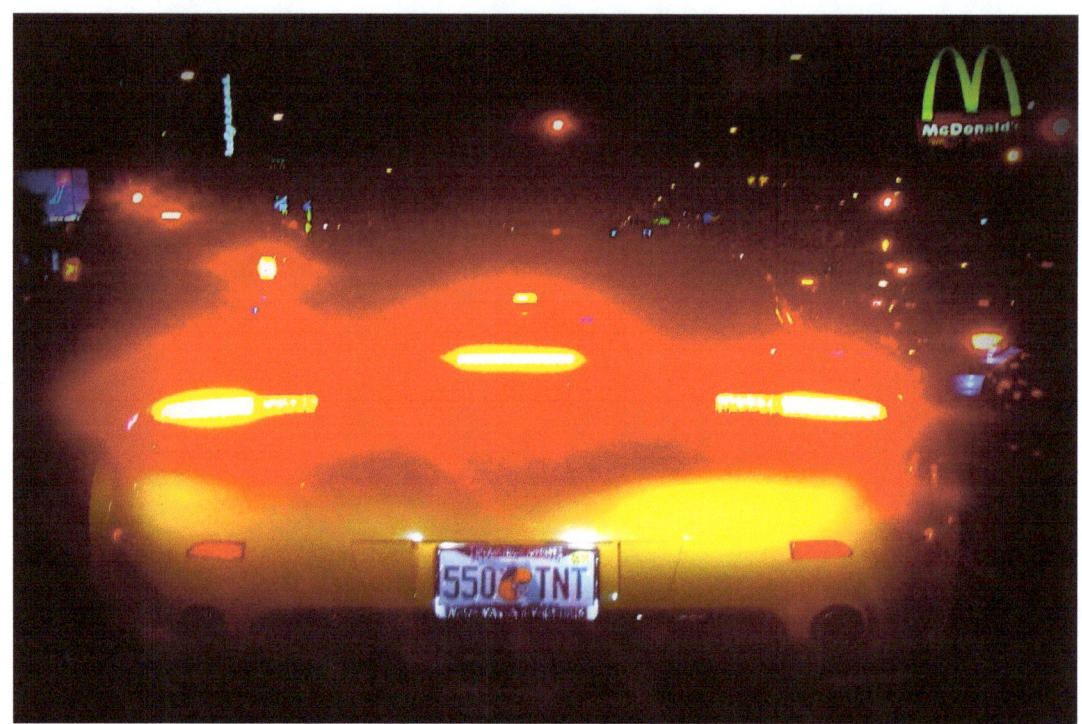

Sunset Blvd.

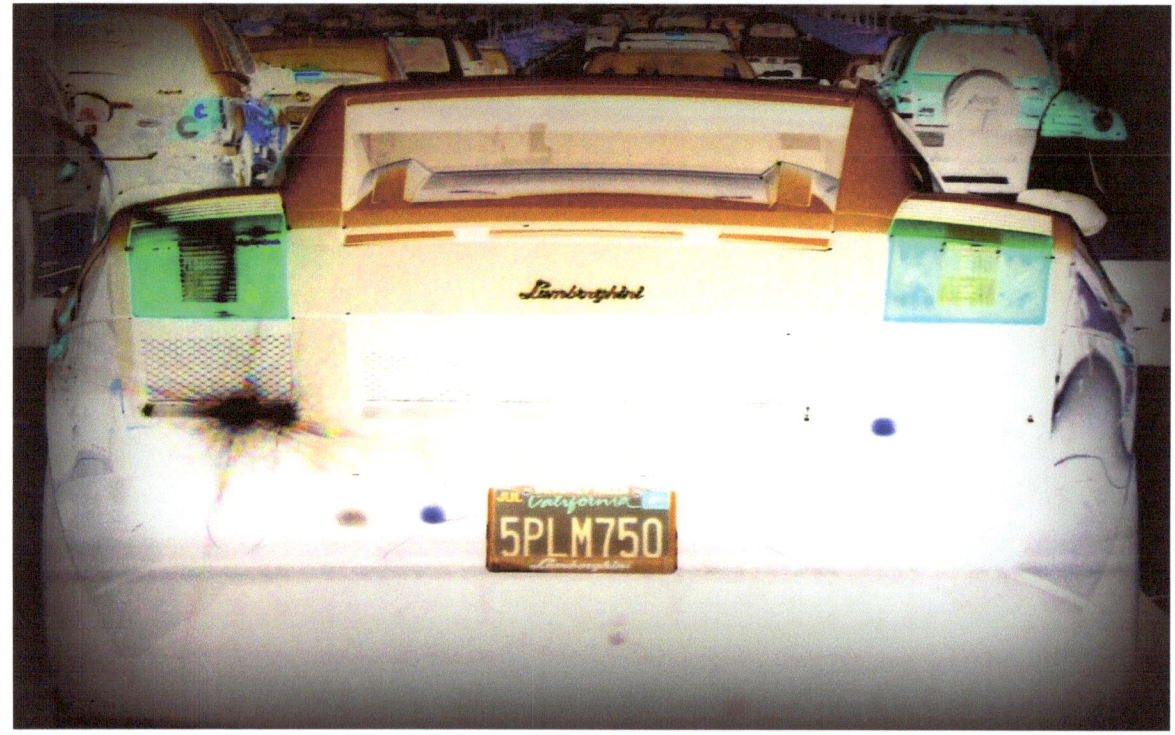

Sunset Blvd II.

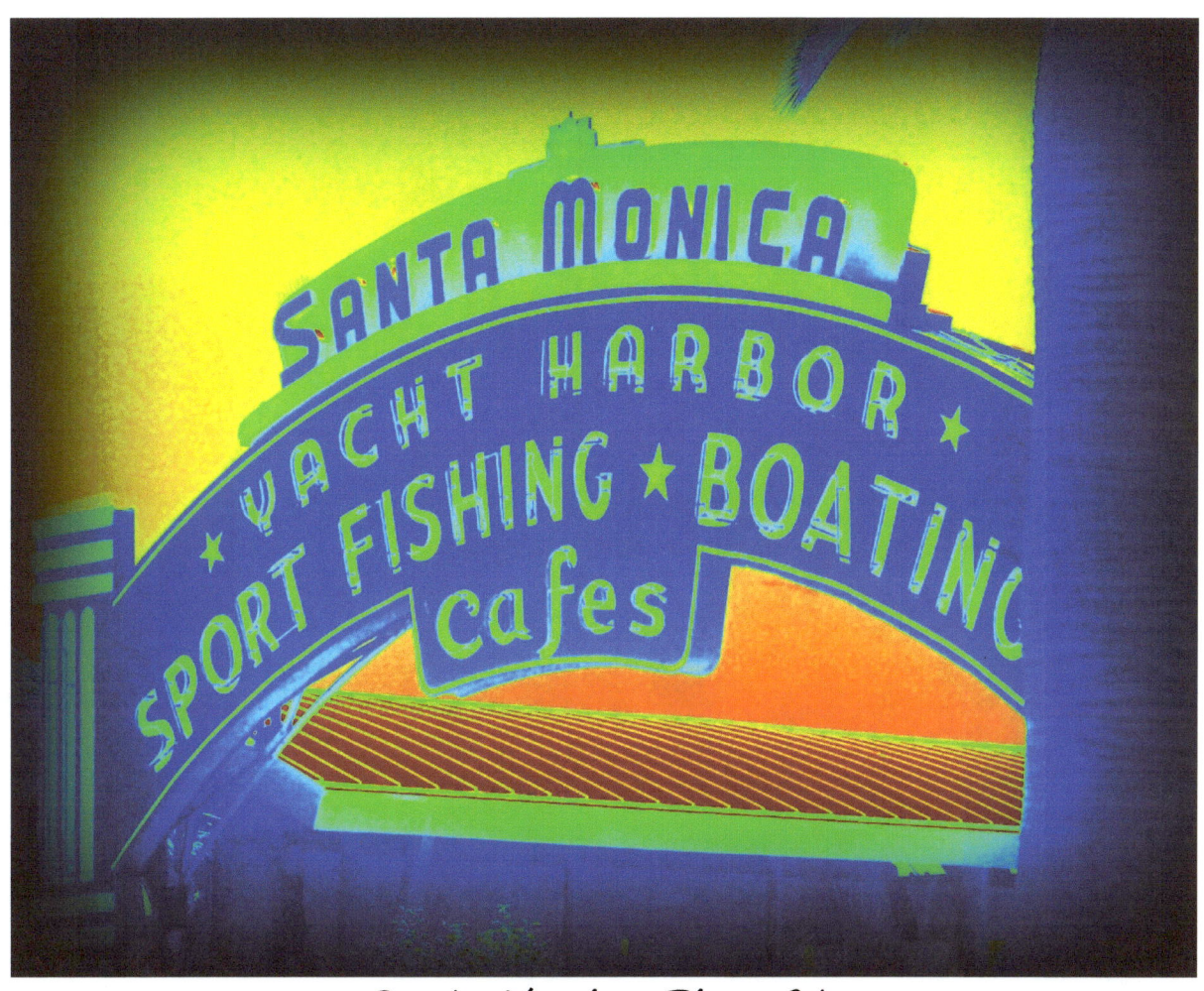

Santa Monica Pier, CA.

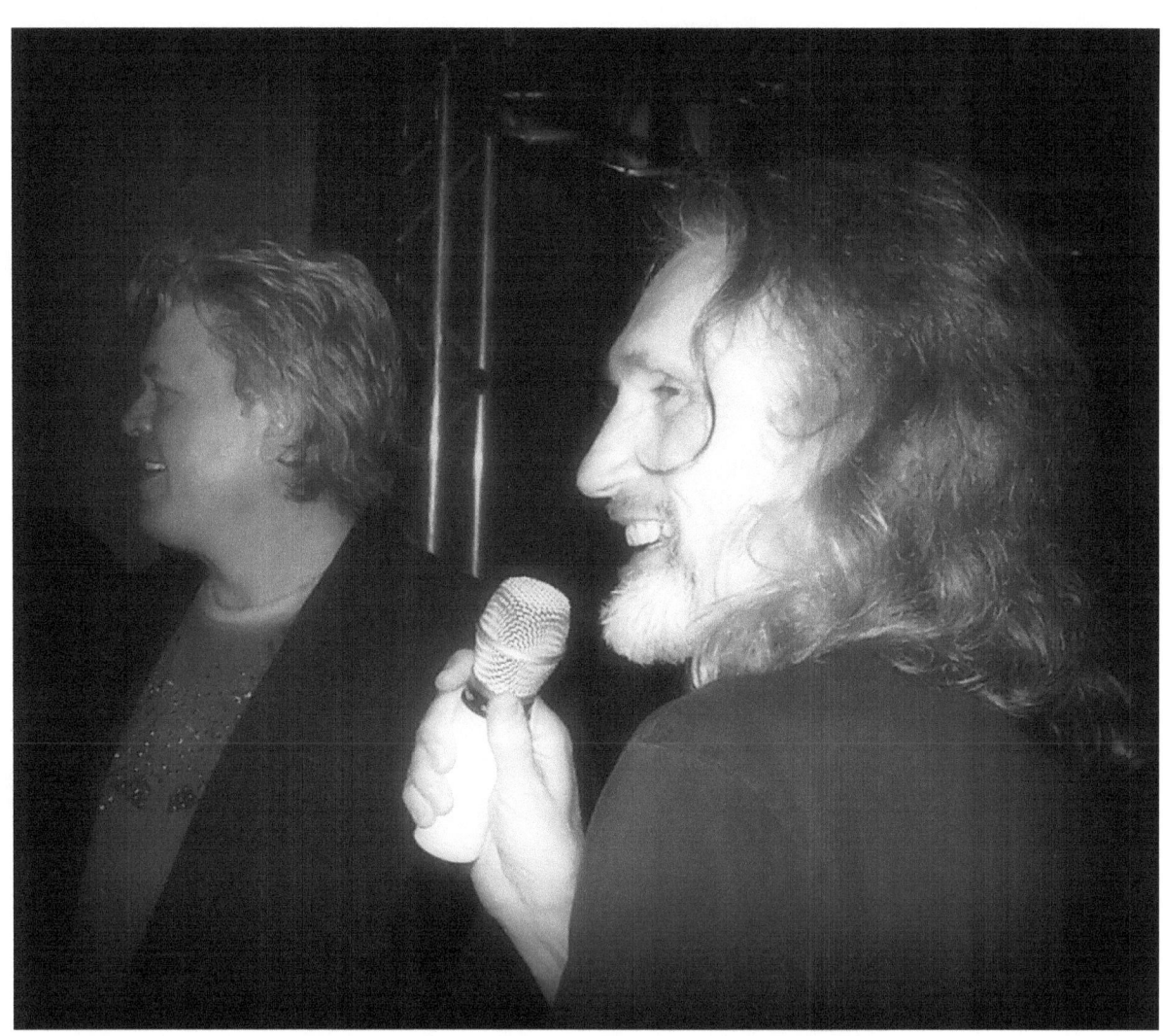

Joey Waldon and Ron White

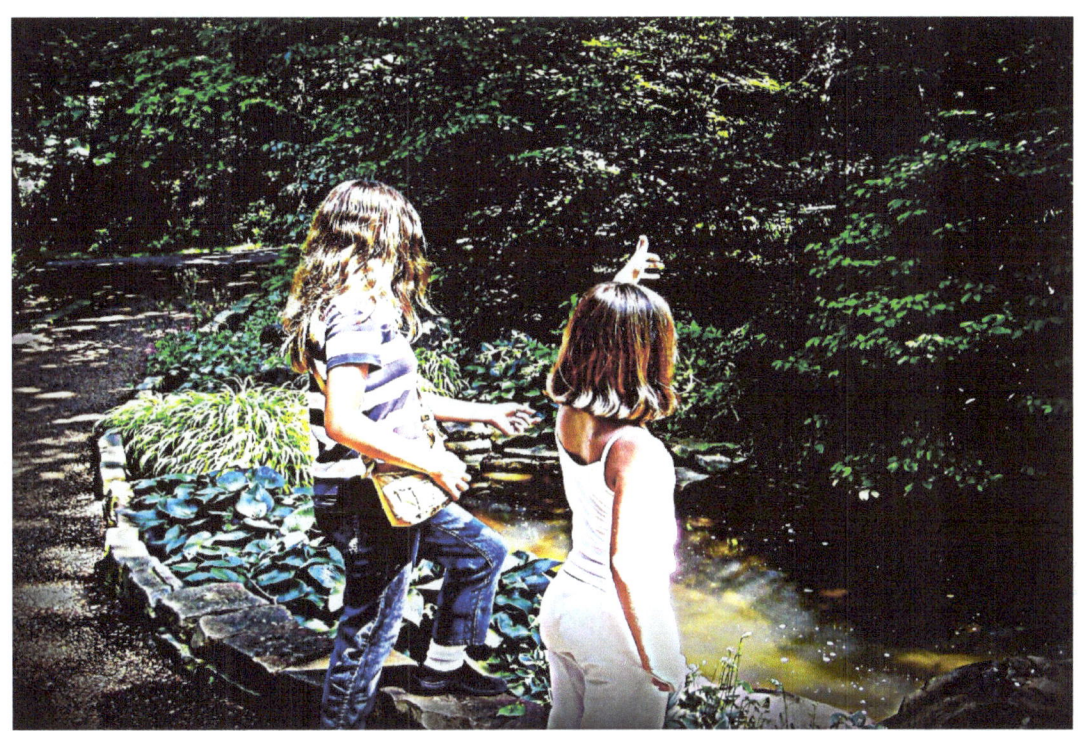

Kids in the Park

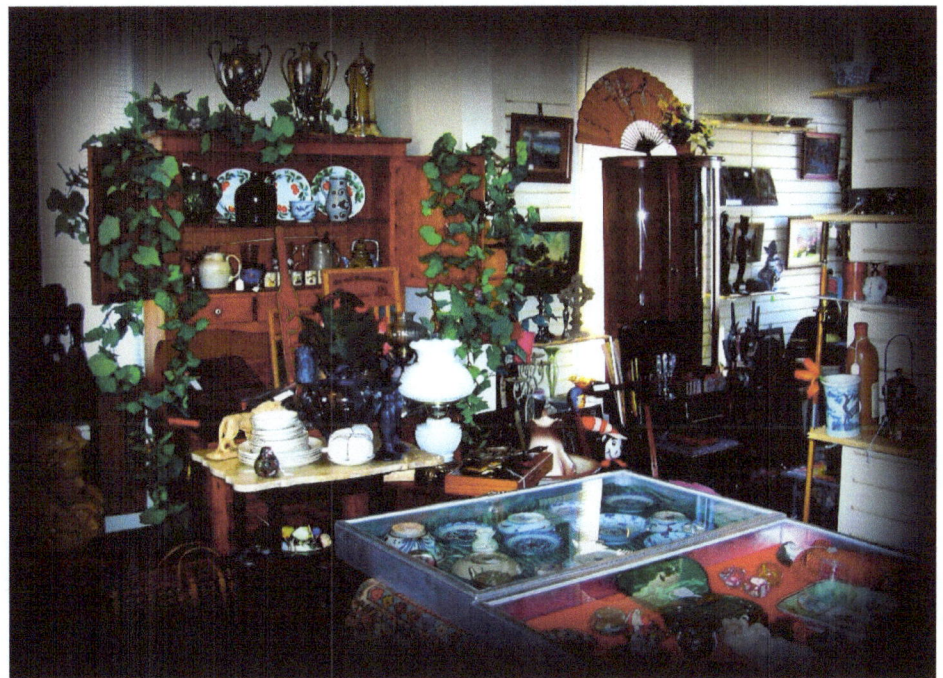

My Old Antique Shop, Westerville, OH.

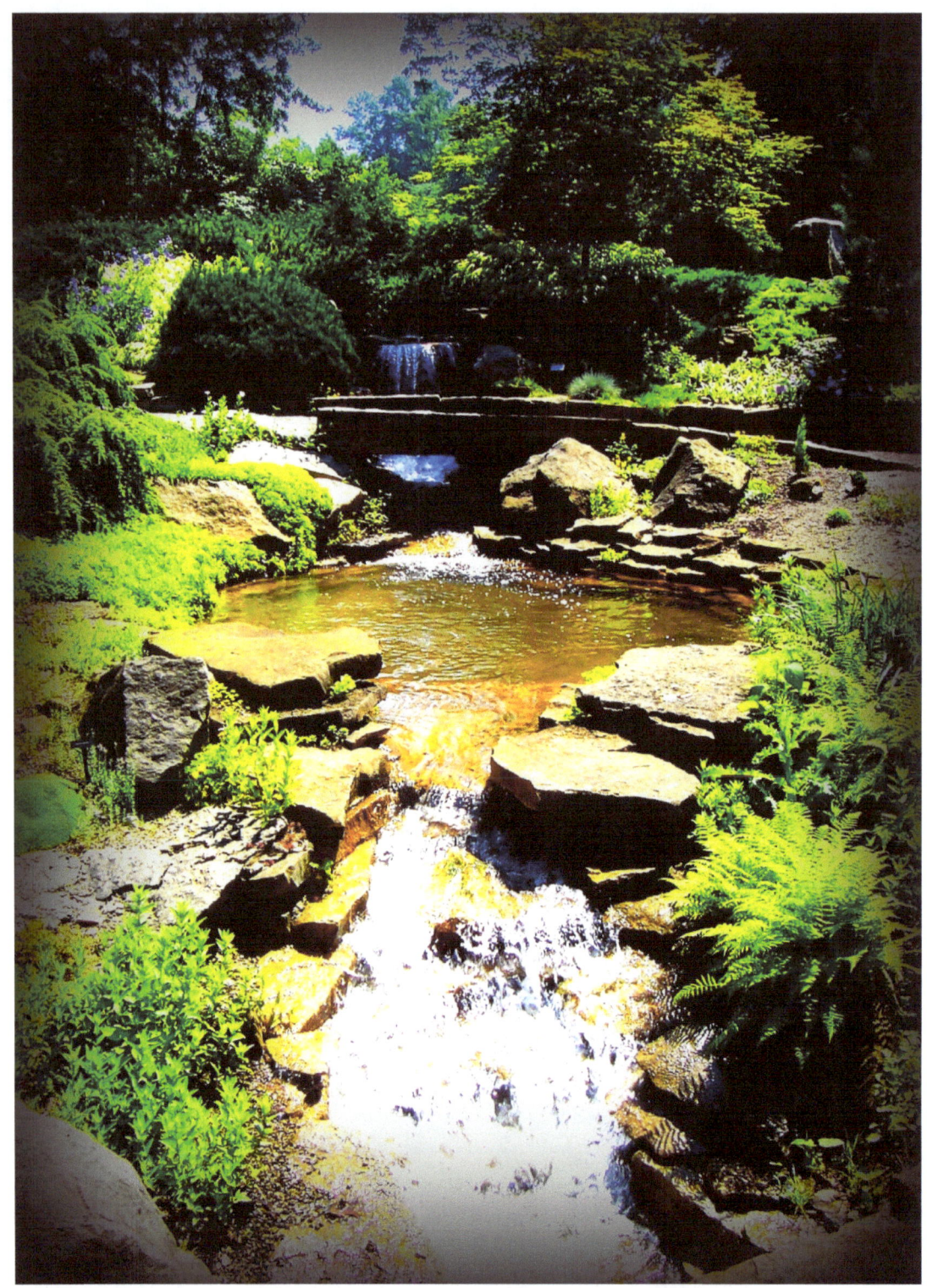

In the Park, Westerville, OH.

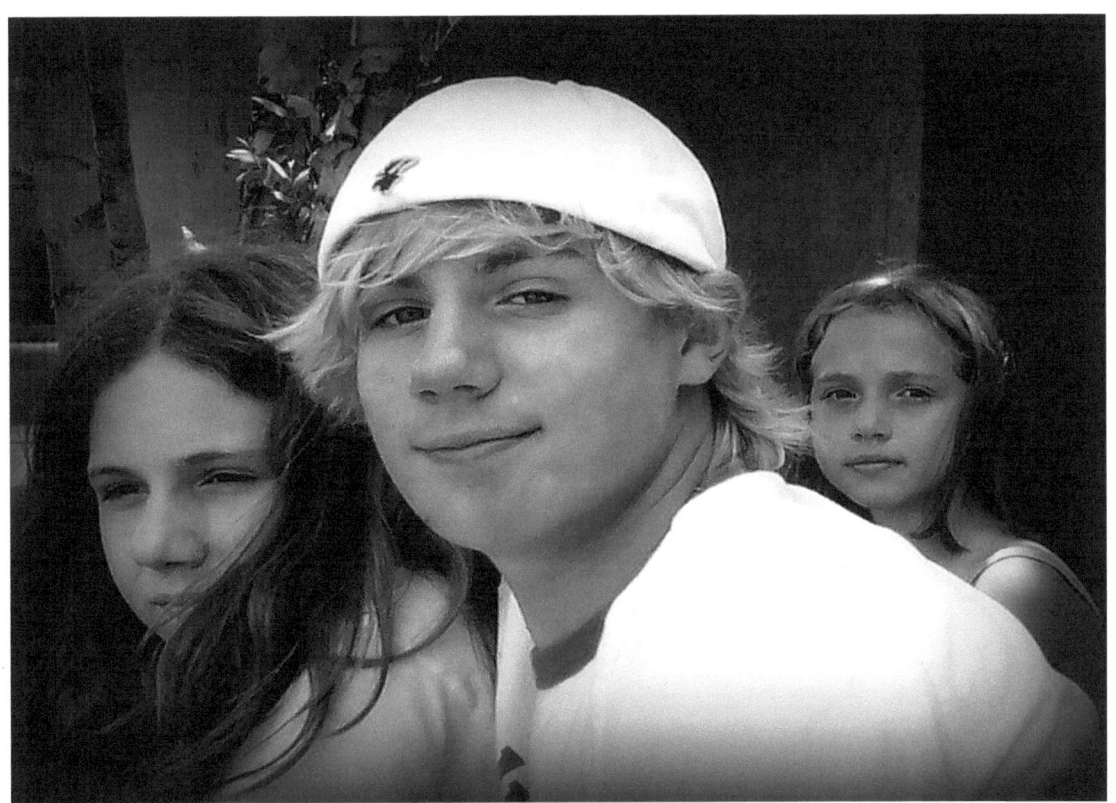

Jack, Lydia, and Alexandra (The Spawn)

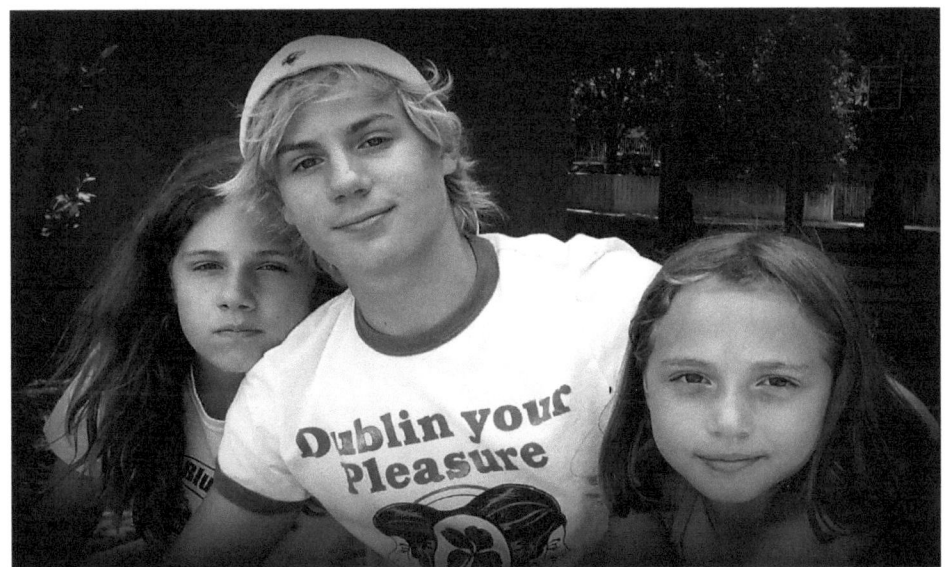

Jack, Lydia, and Alexandra (The Spawn) II

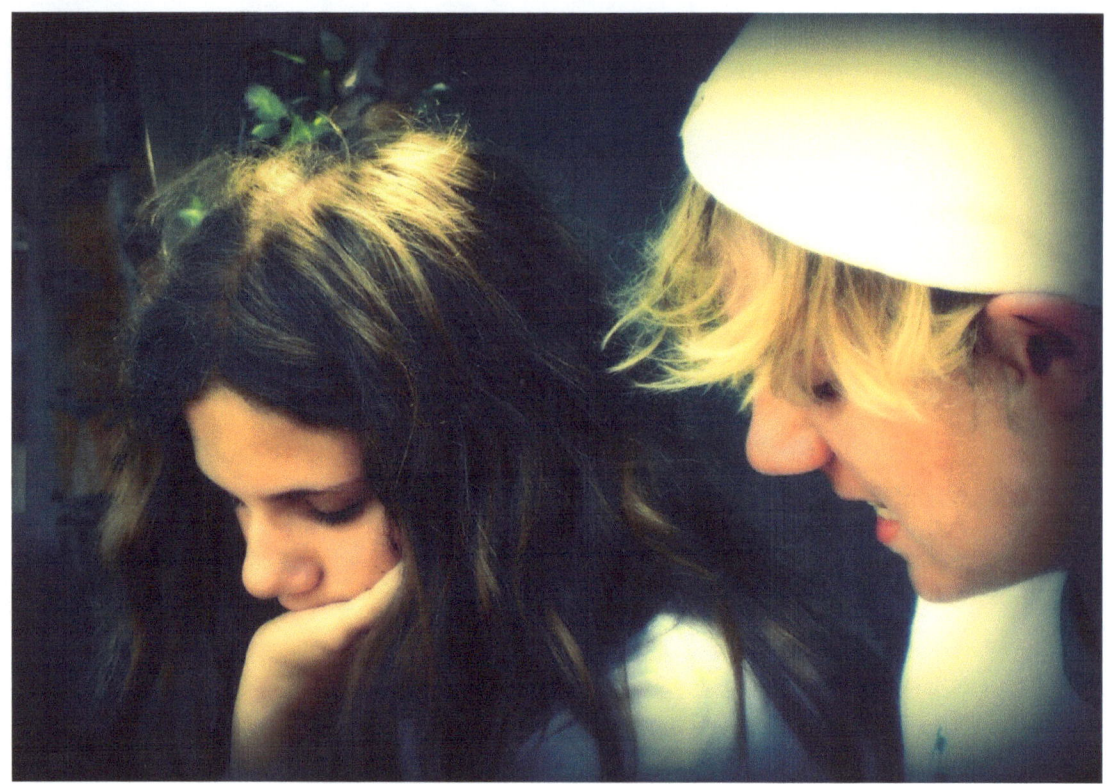

Jack and Lydia

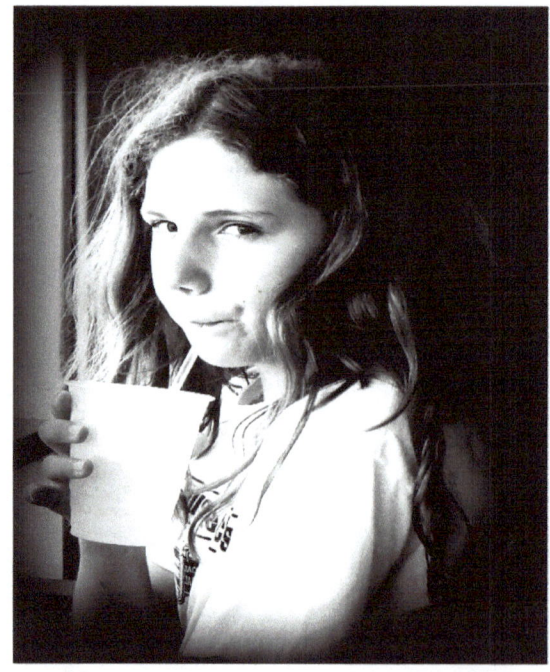

Lydia Drinking Furtively

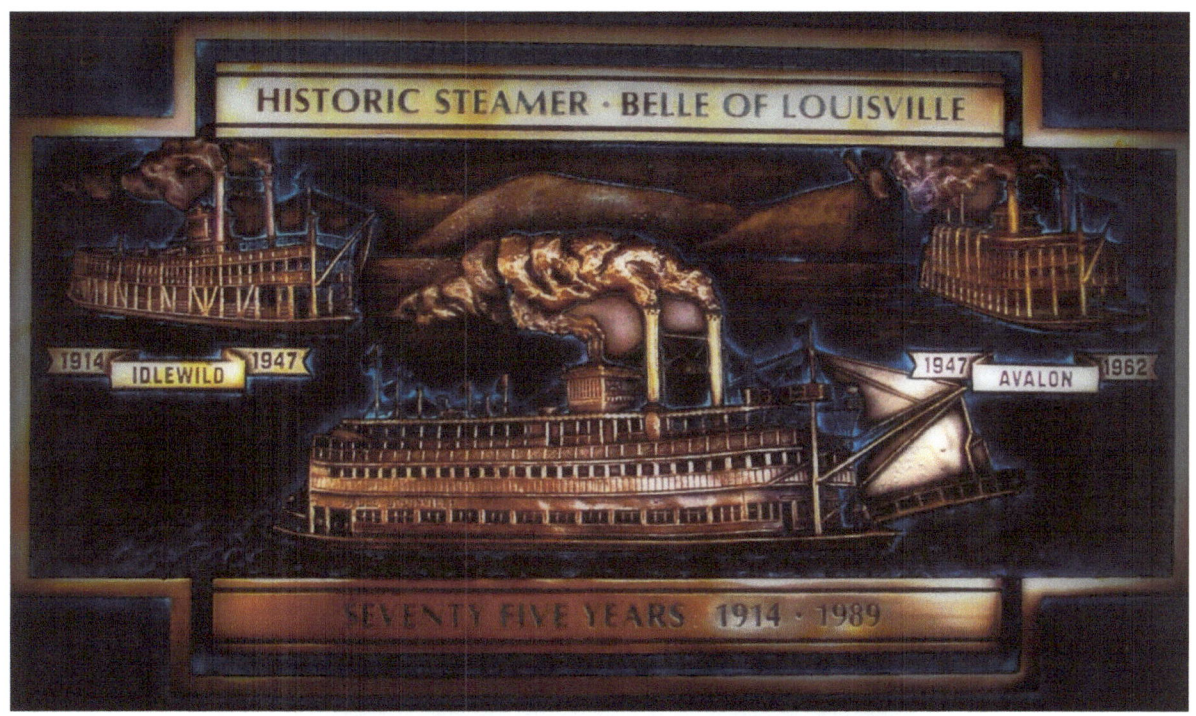

St. Louis, Paddle Steamer

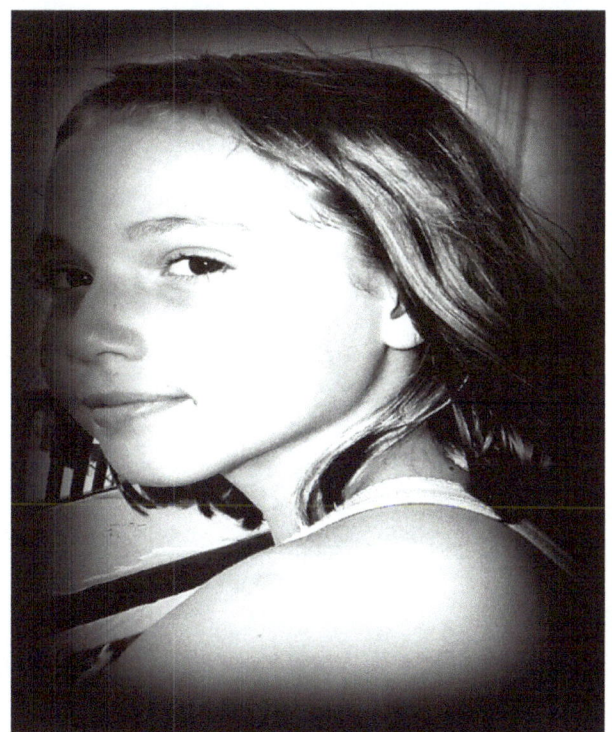

Alex

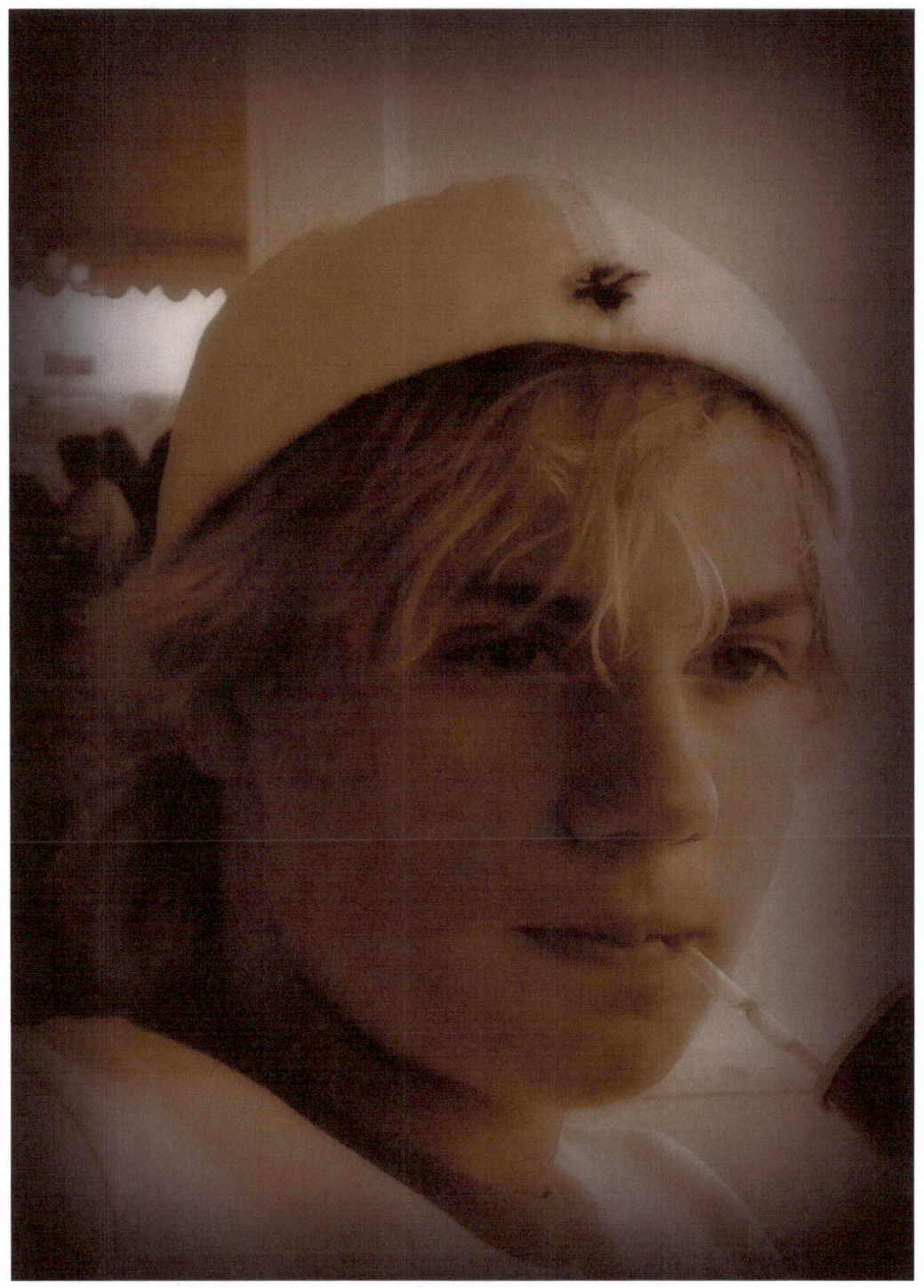

Jack

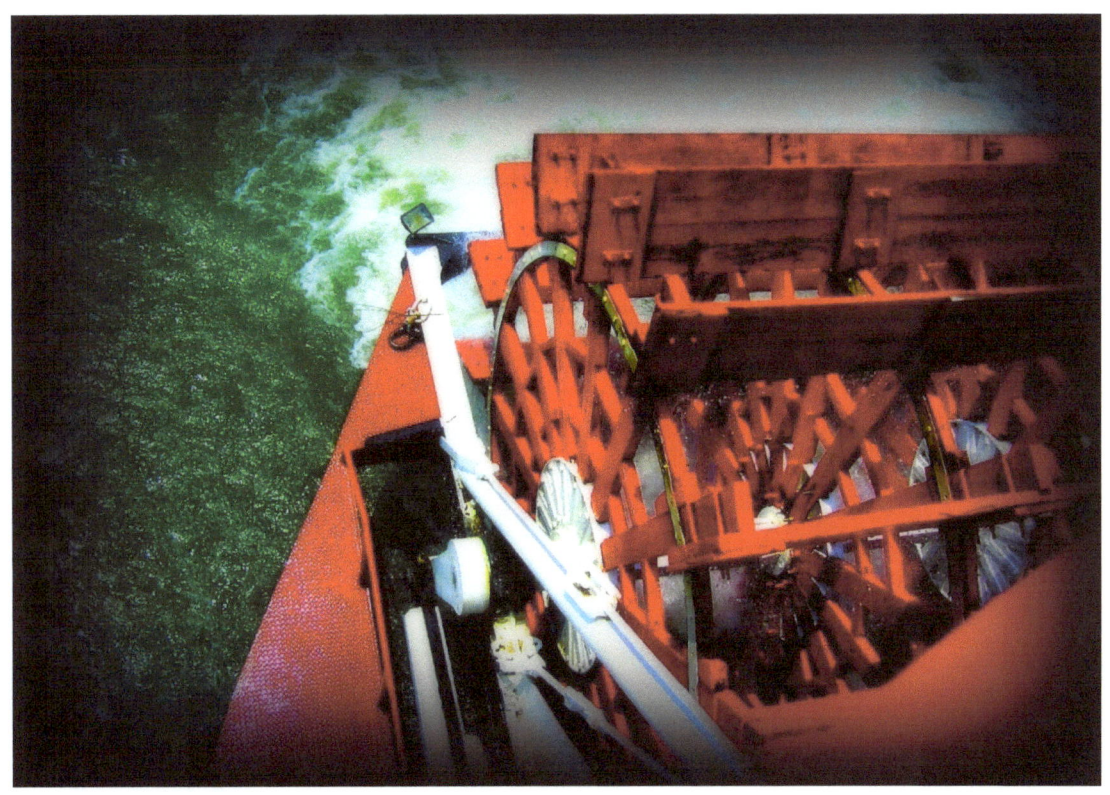

Paddle Steamer

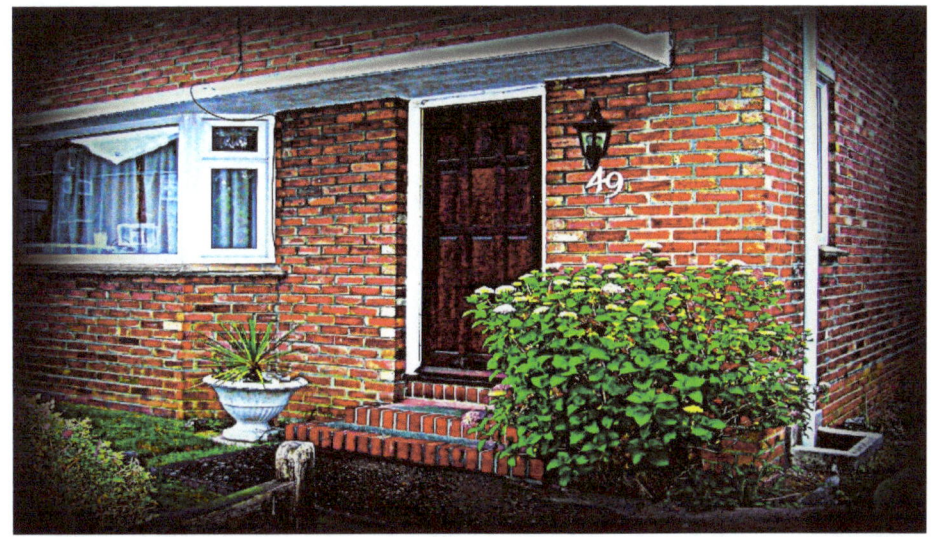

49 Cumberland

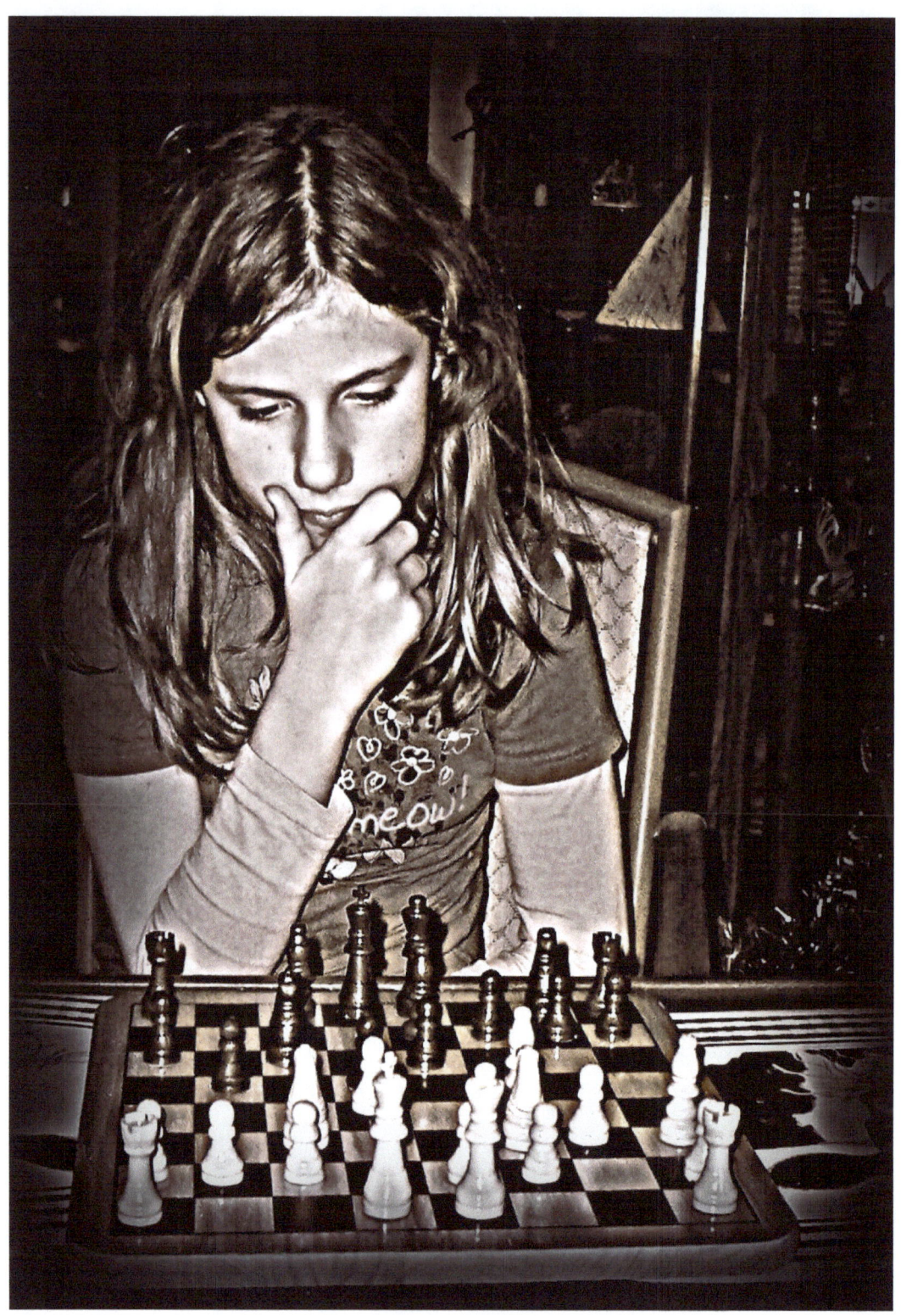

Mmmmm...

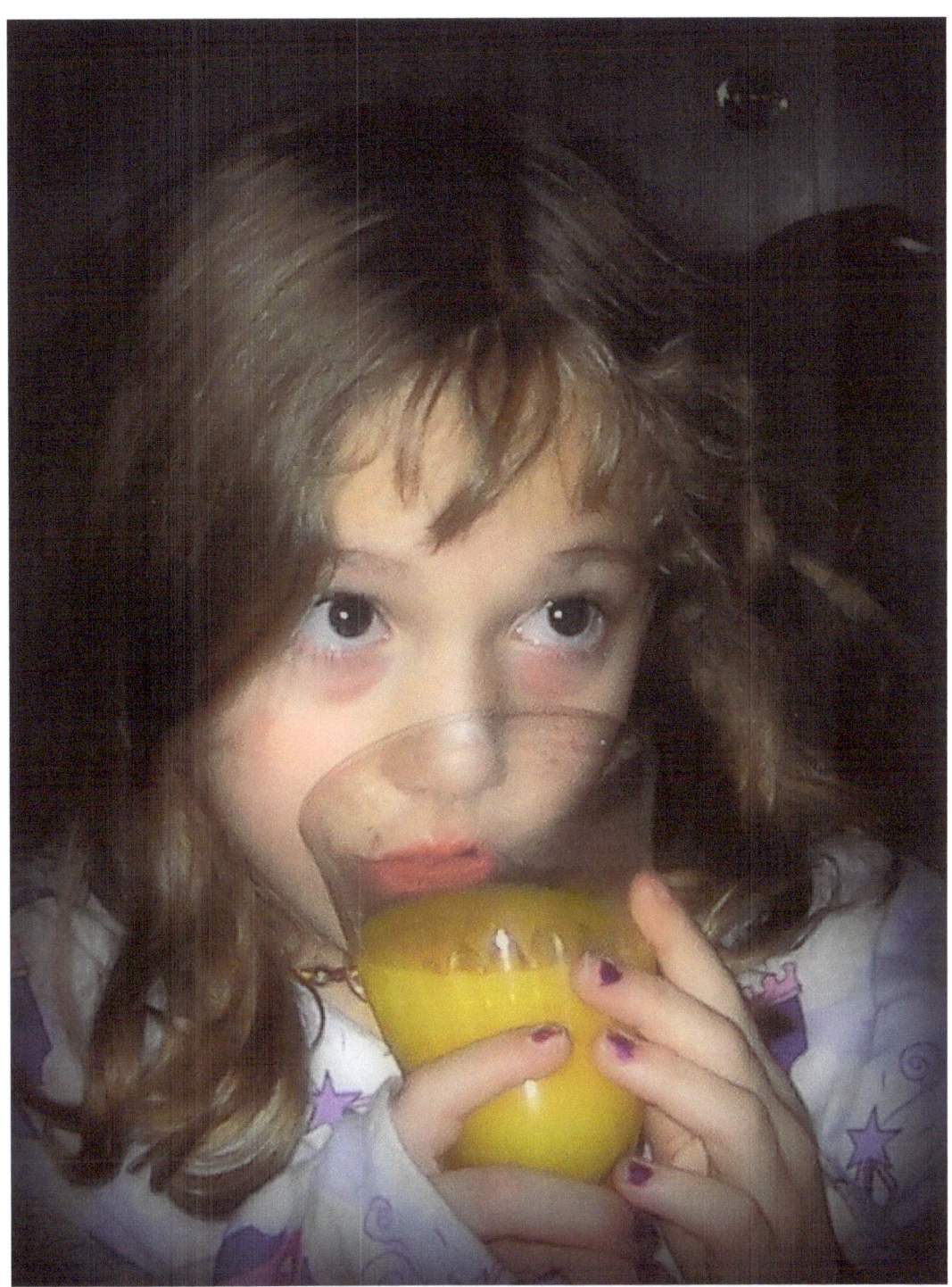

It Needs Some More Gin...

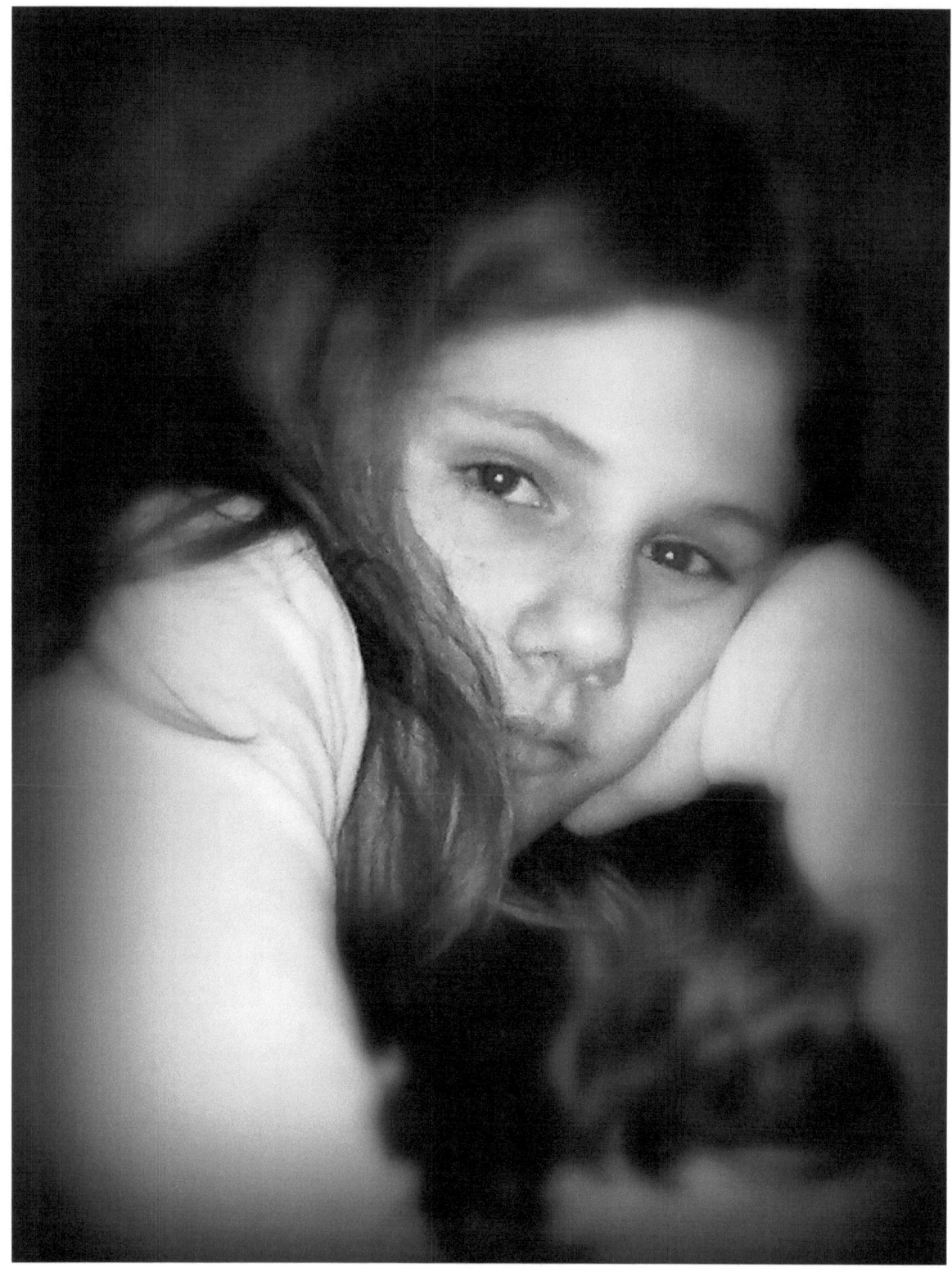

Lydia

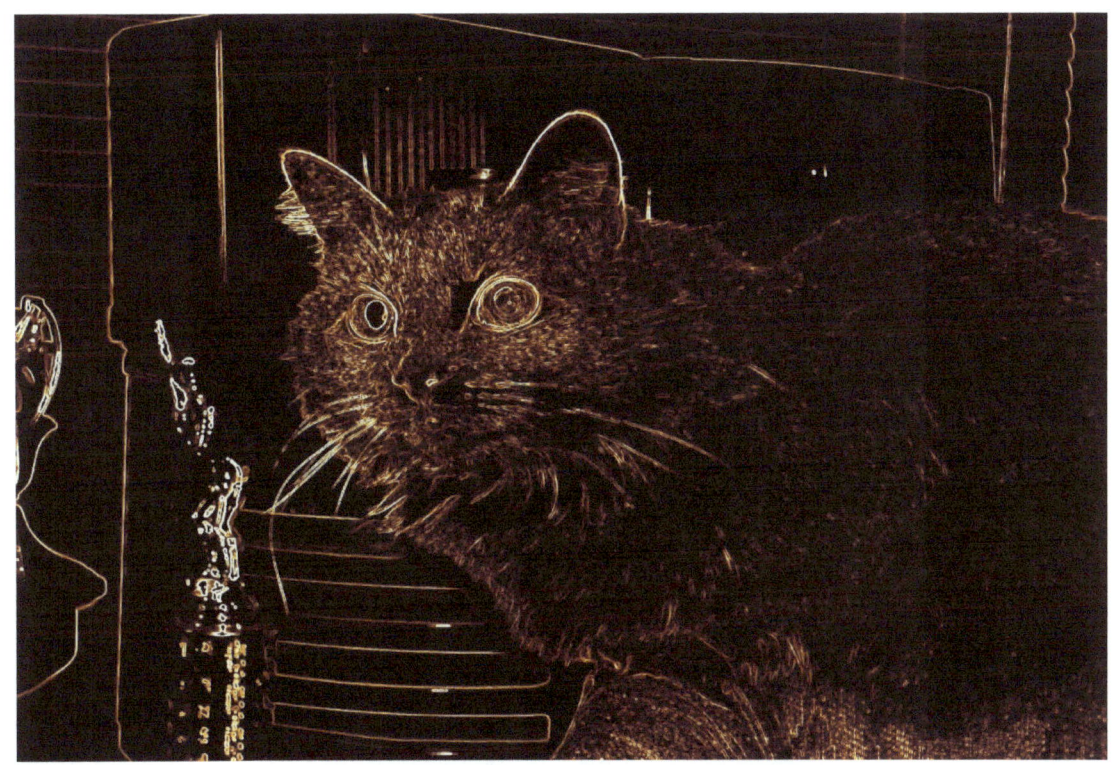

The Terror Muppet

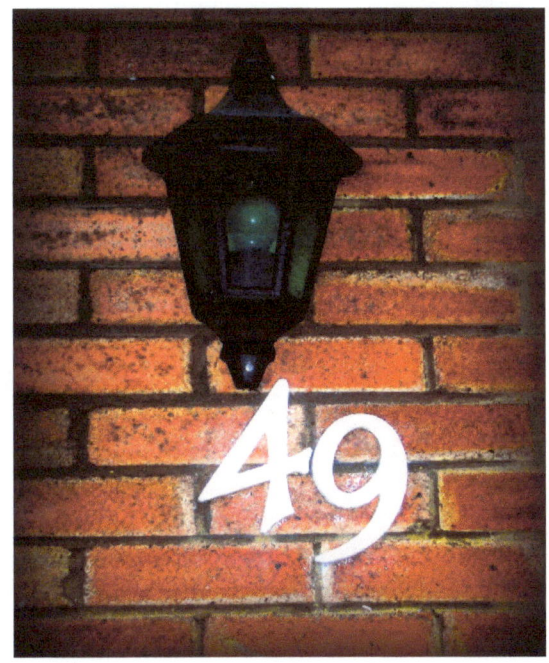

49

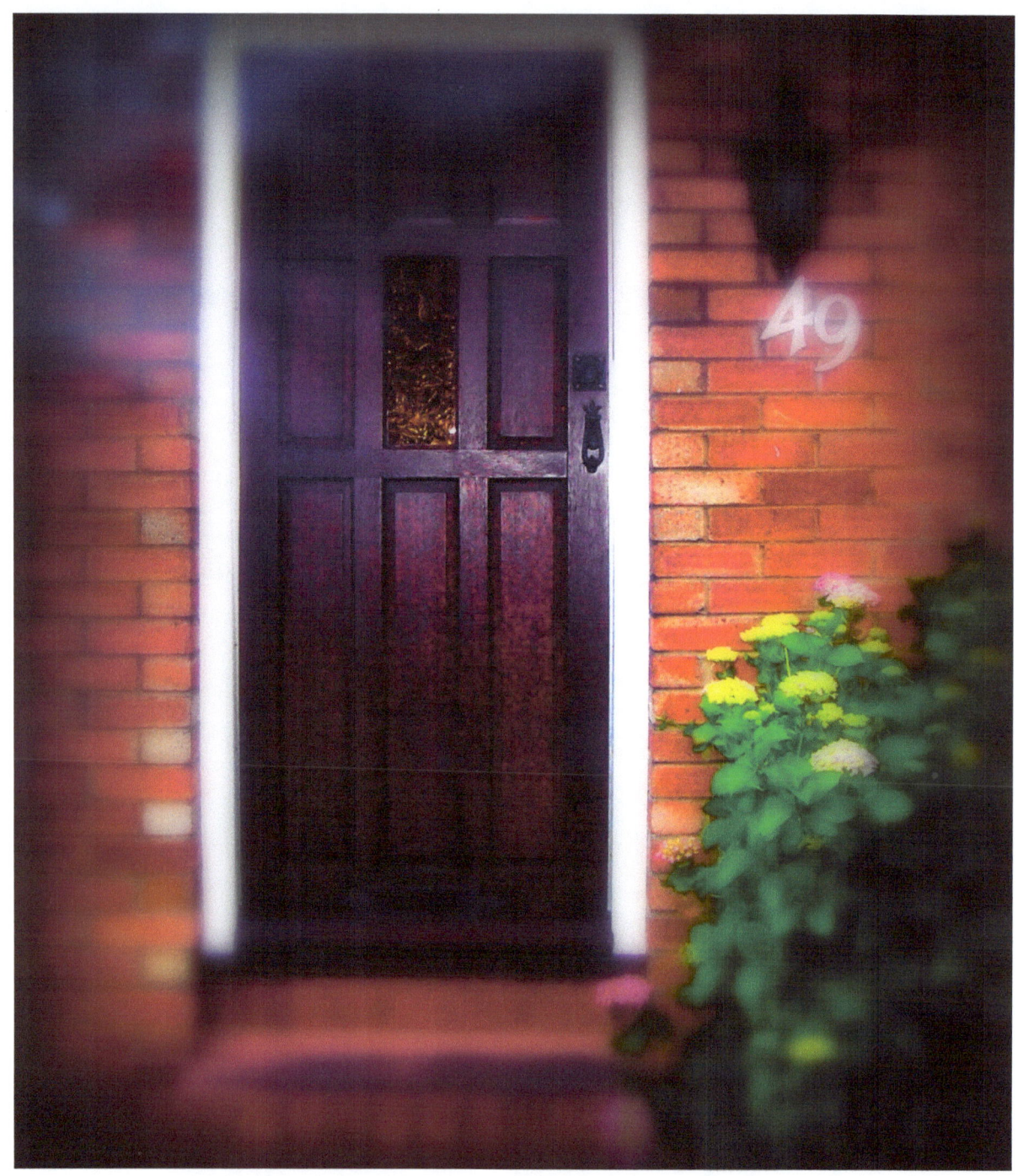

49 Cumberland Crescent, Chelmsford, Essex

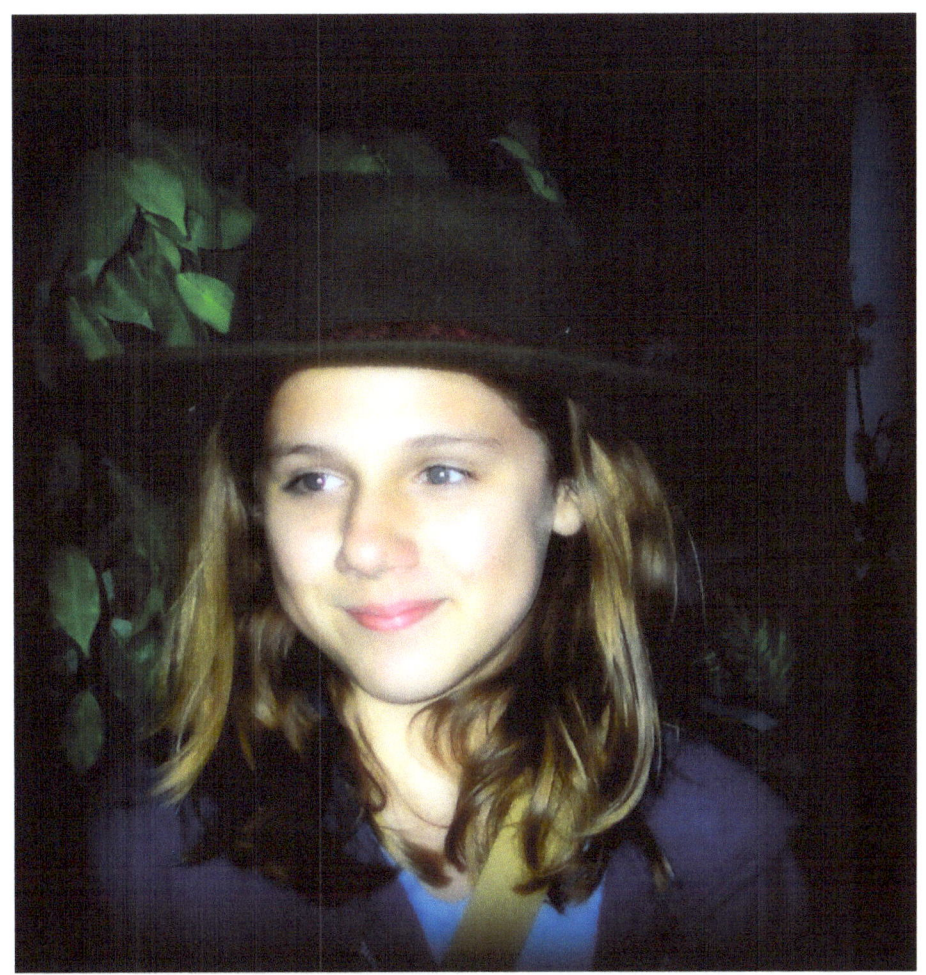

Lydia

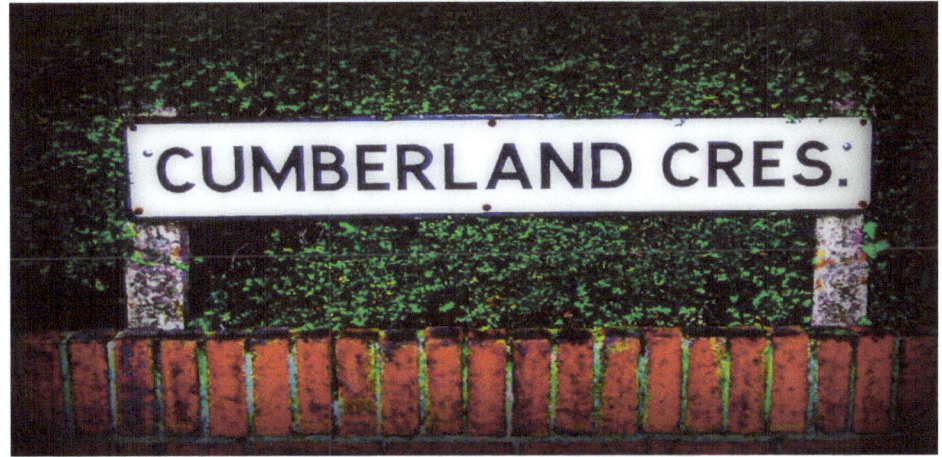

Cumberland Crescent

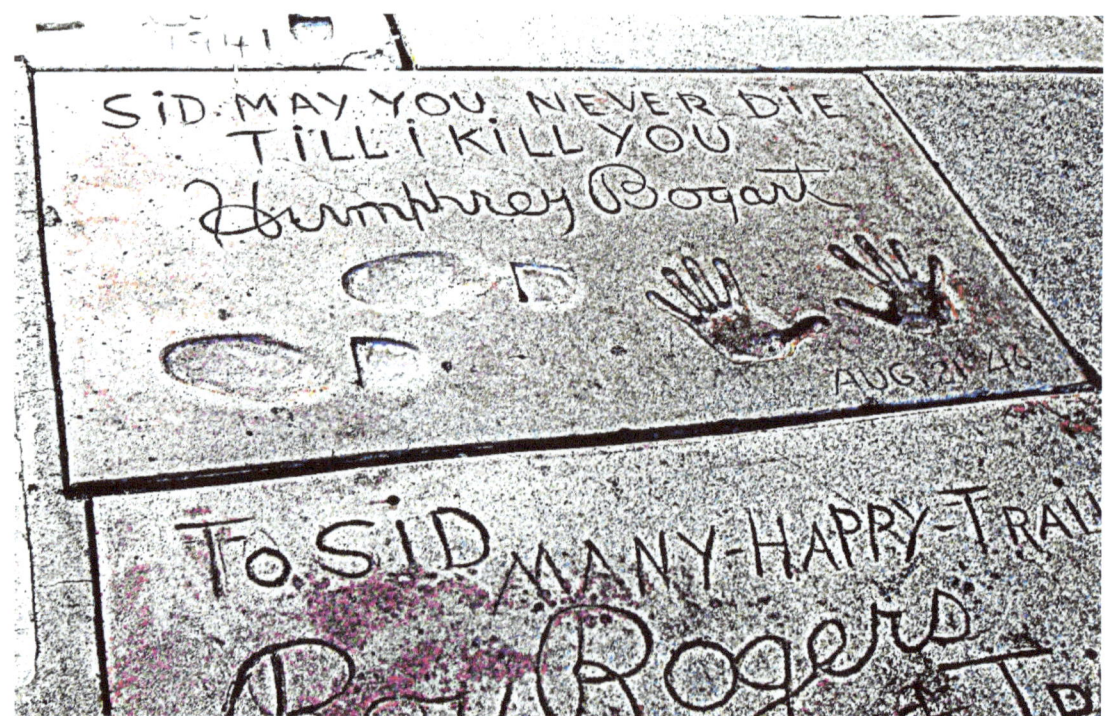

Grauman's Chinese Theater

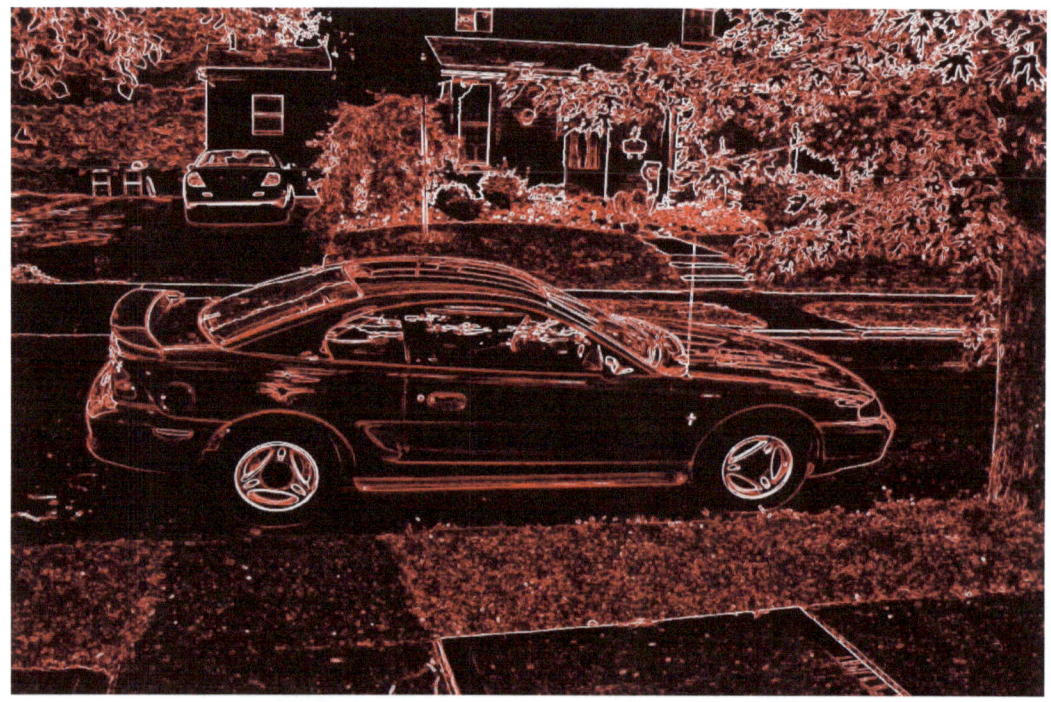

My Old Mustang – RIP

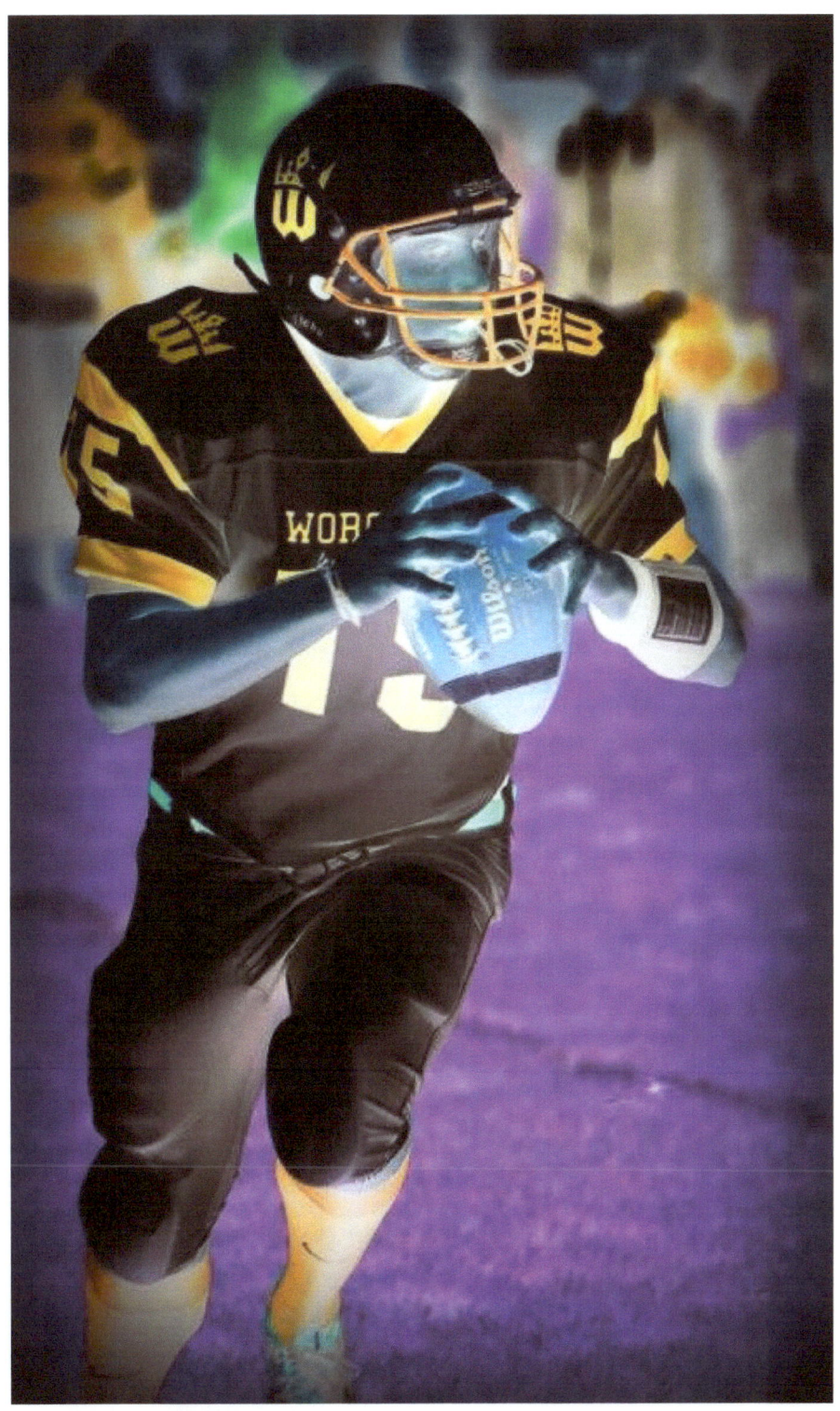

Jack, Worcester Royals Quarterback

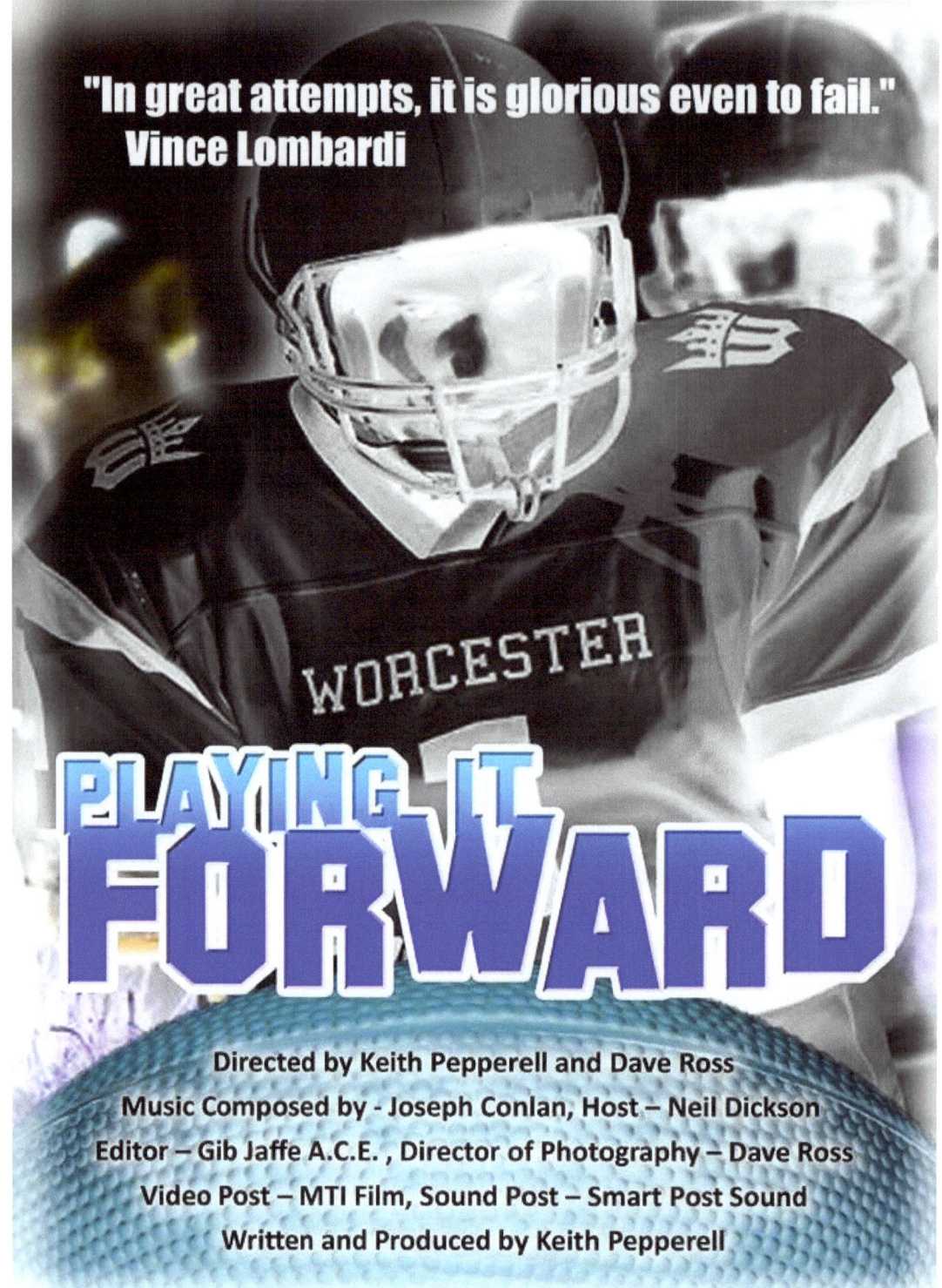

Playing it Forward, IMDB Poster

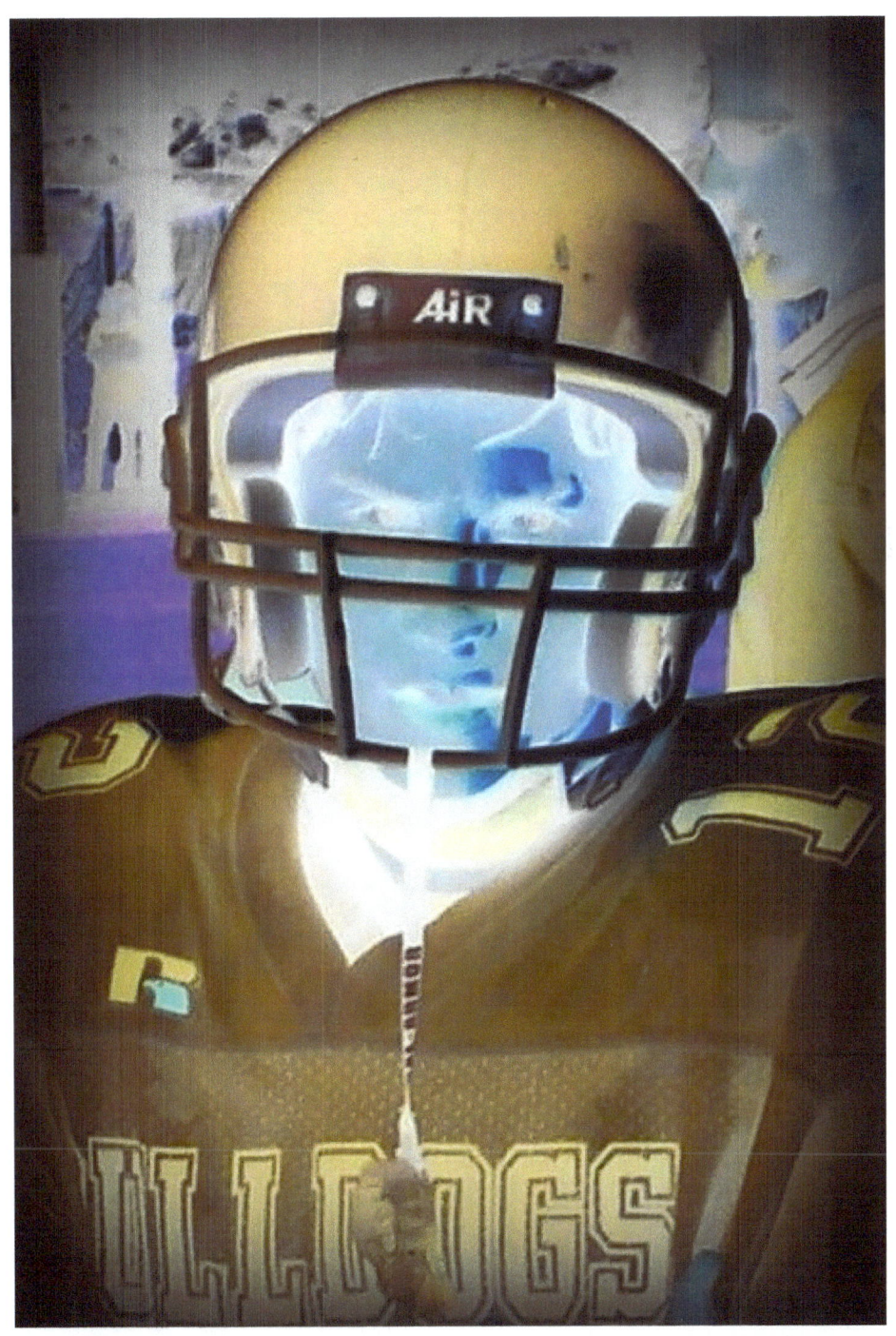

Jack, a Bulldog

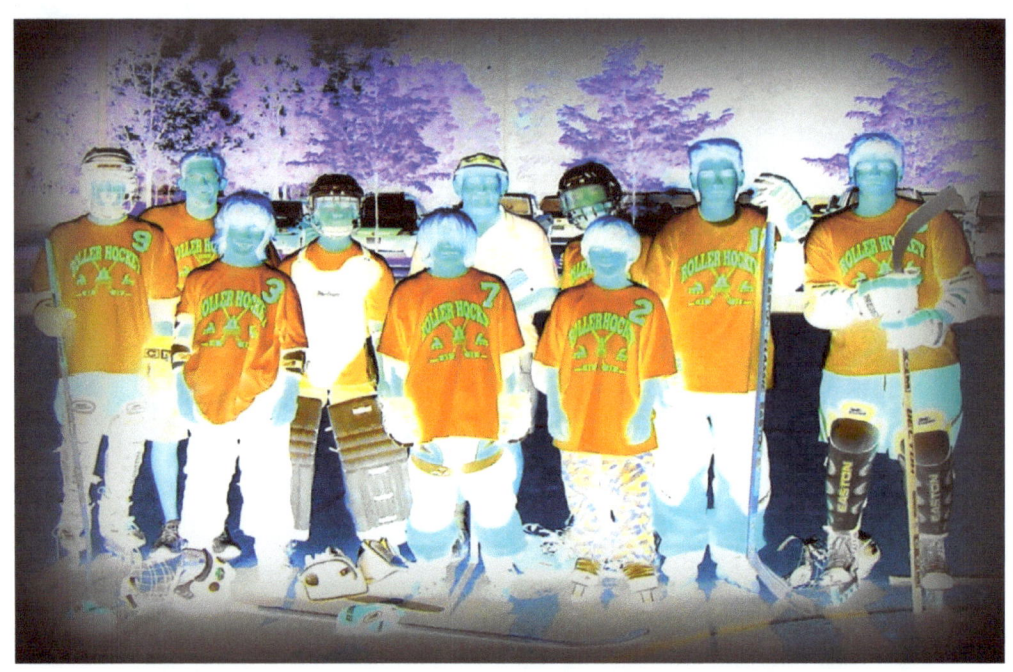

Roller Blade Dudes

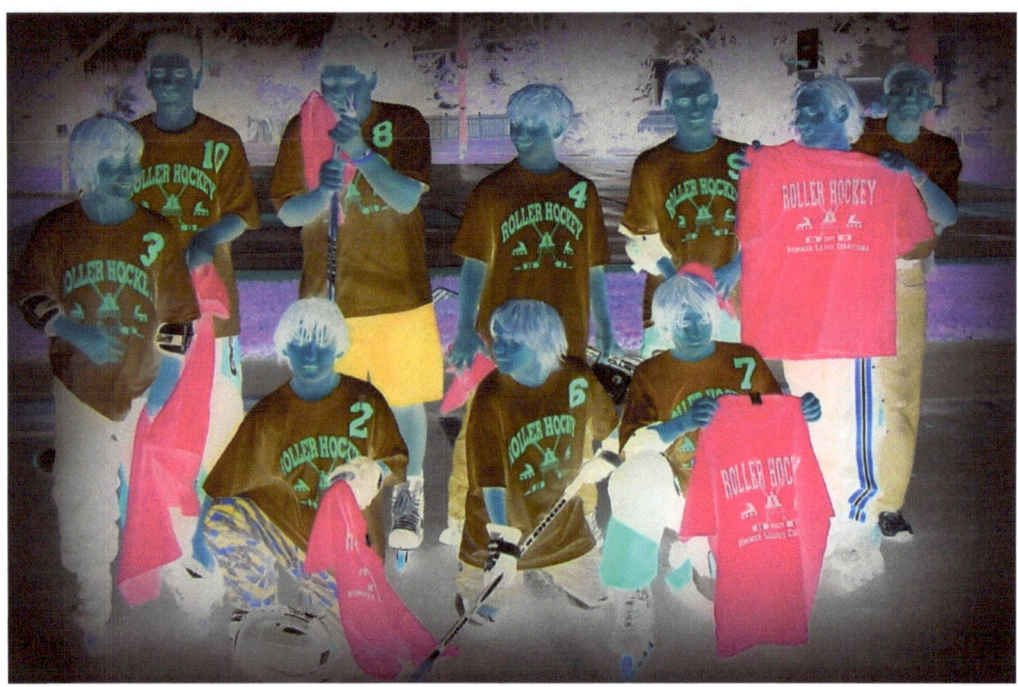

League Champions!

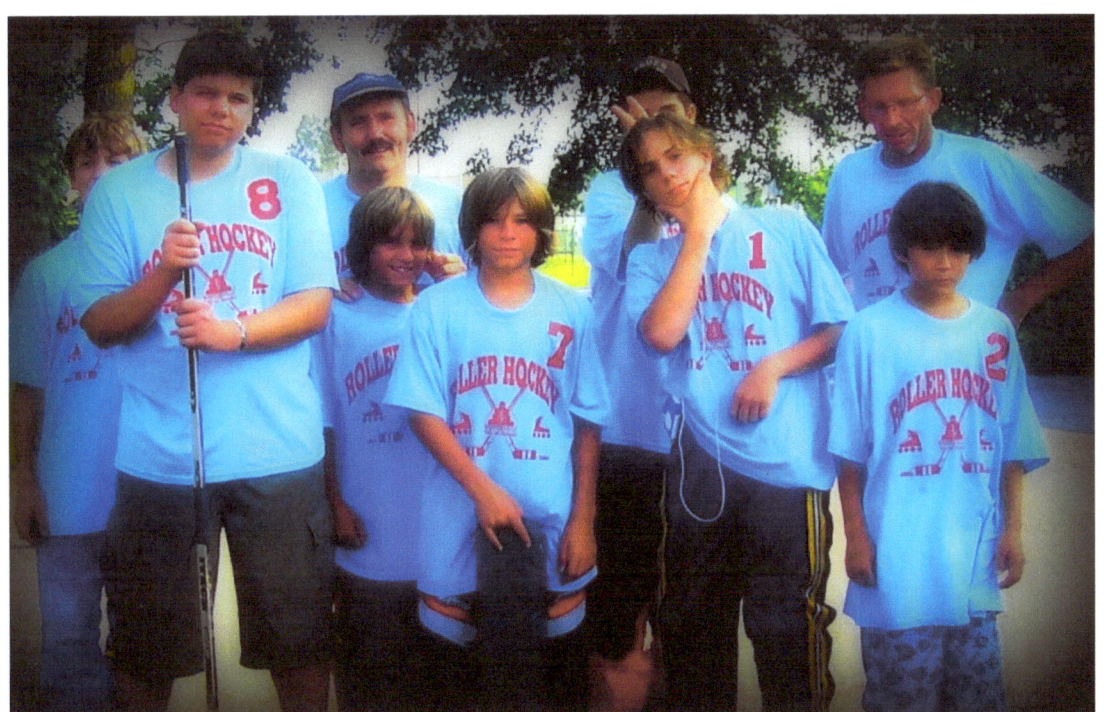

A Very Motley Crew

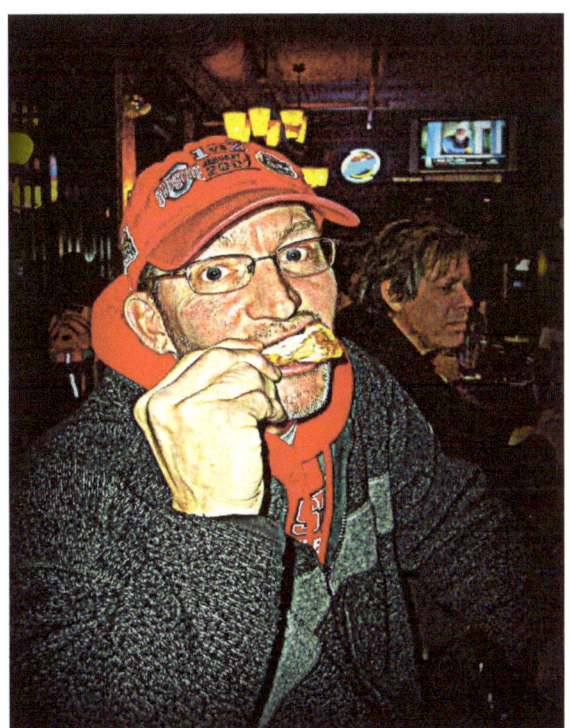

Creature from the Wing Lagoon

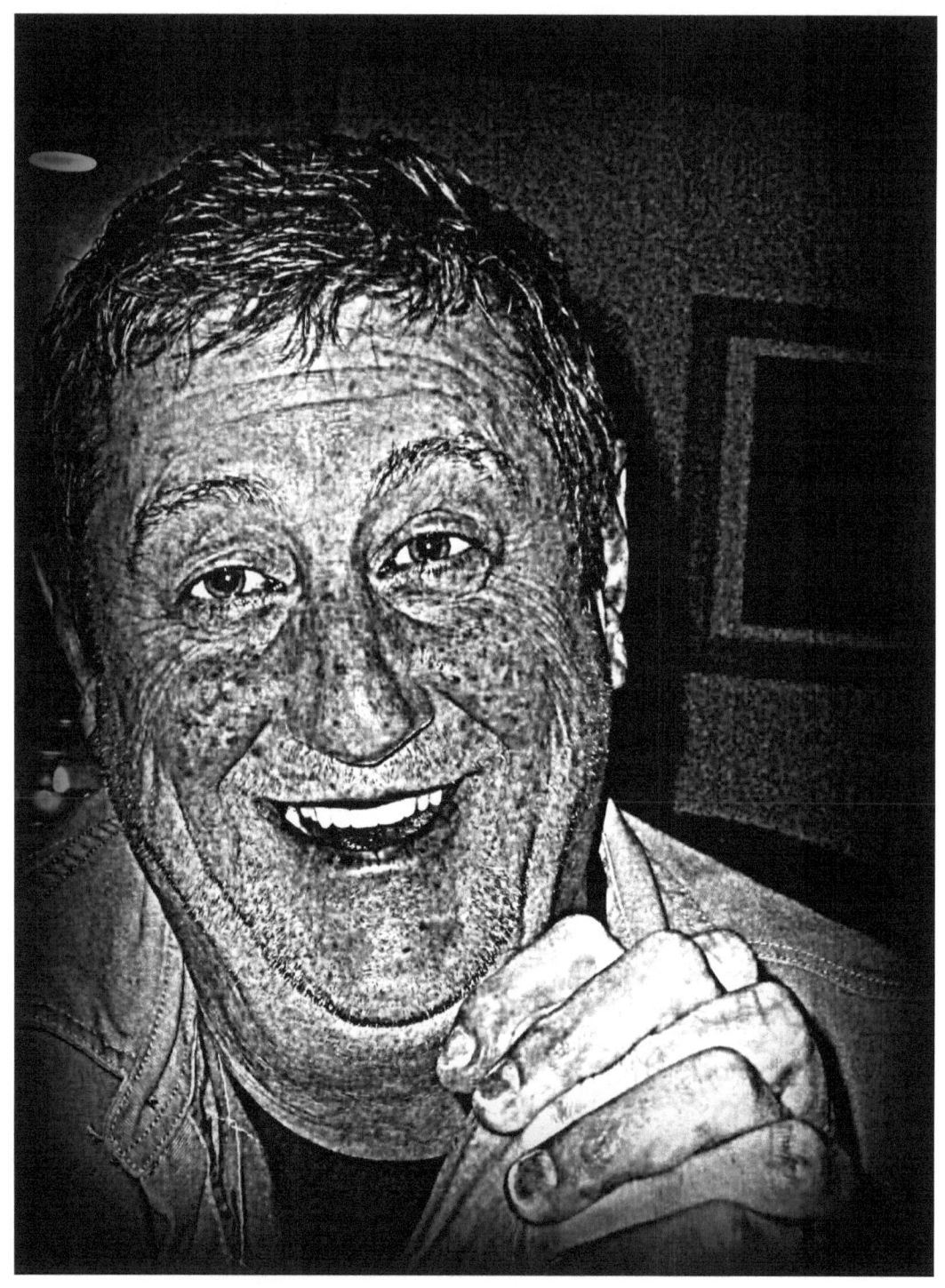

Fred Gwynne ?

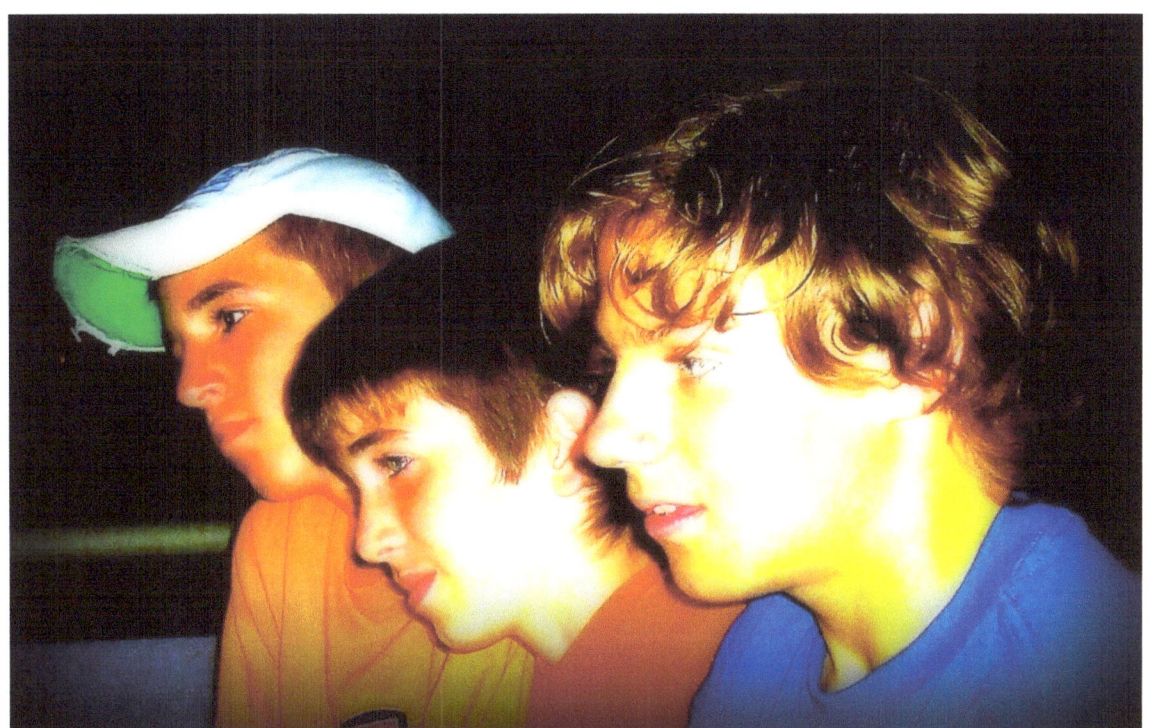

Ben, Judson, and Jack

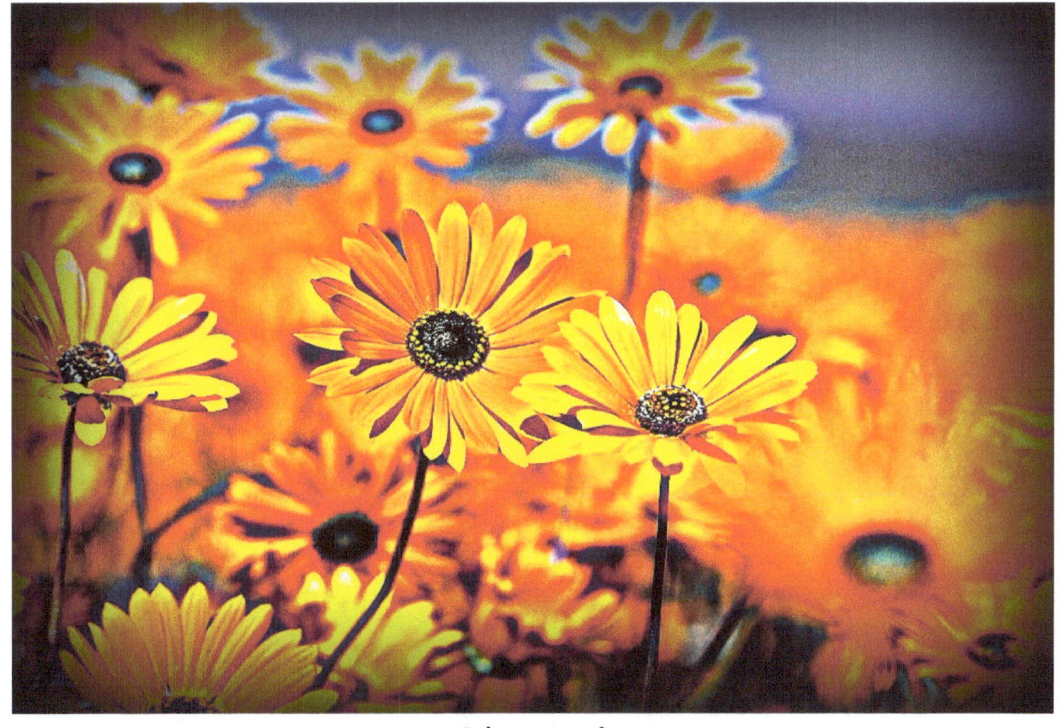

Blooming

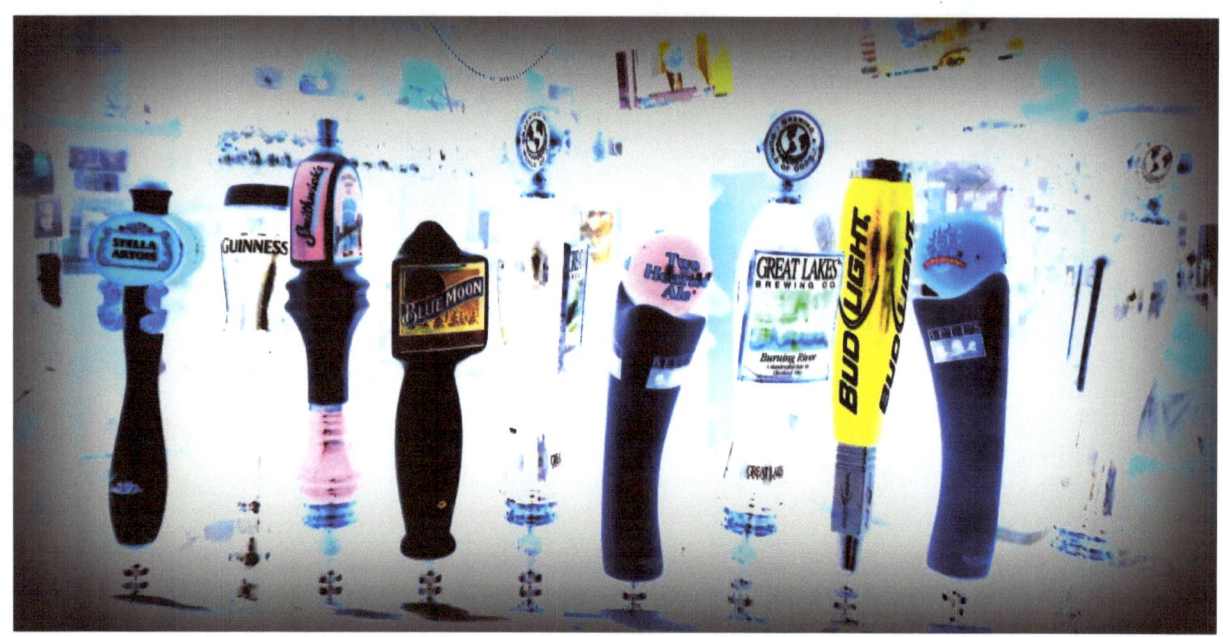

Getting Pumped

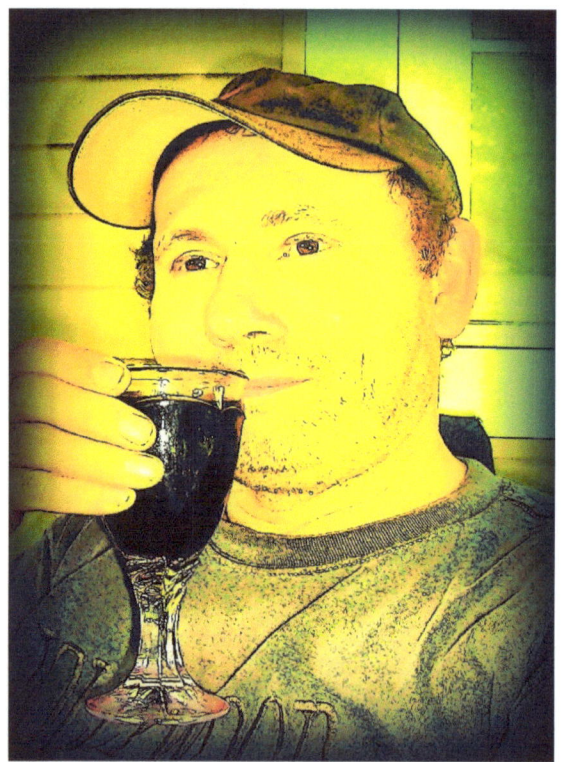

A Large Moistener

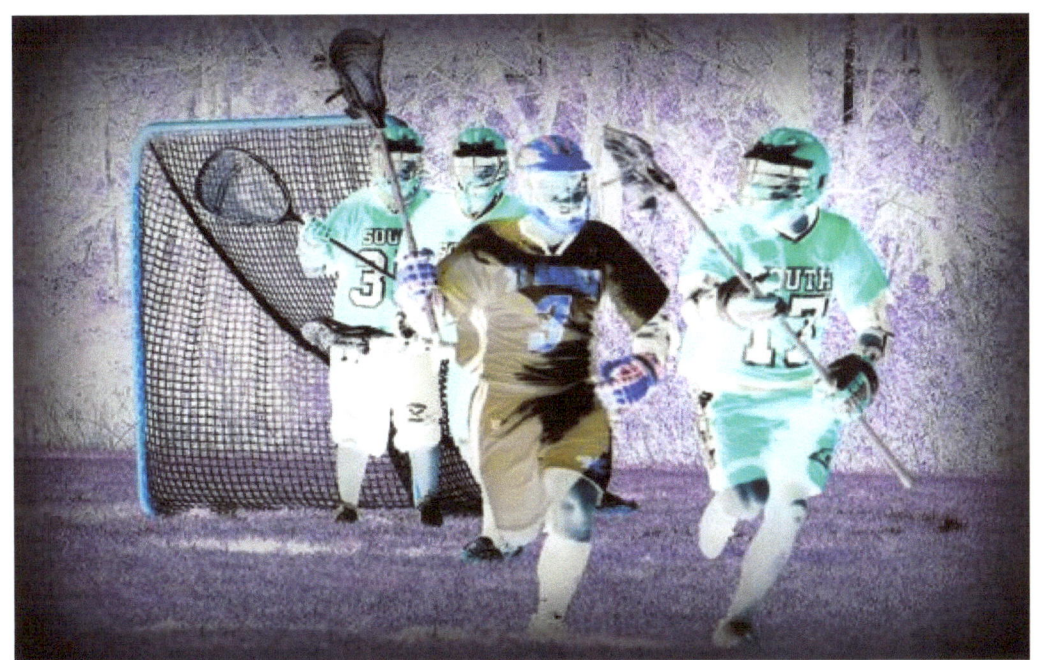

South HS, LAX

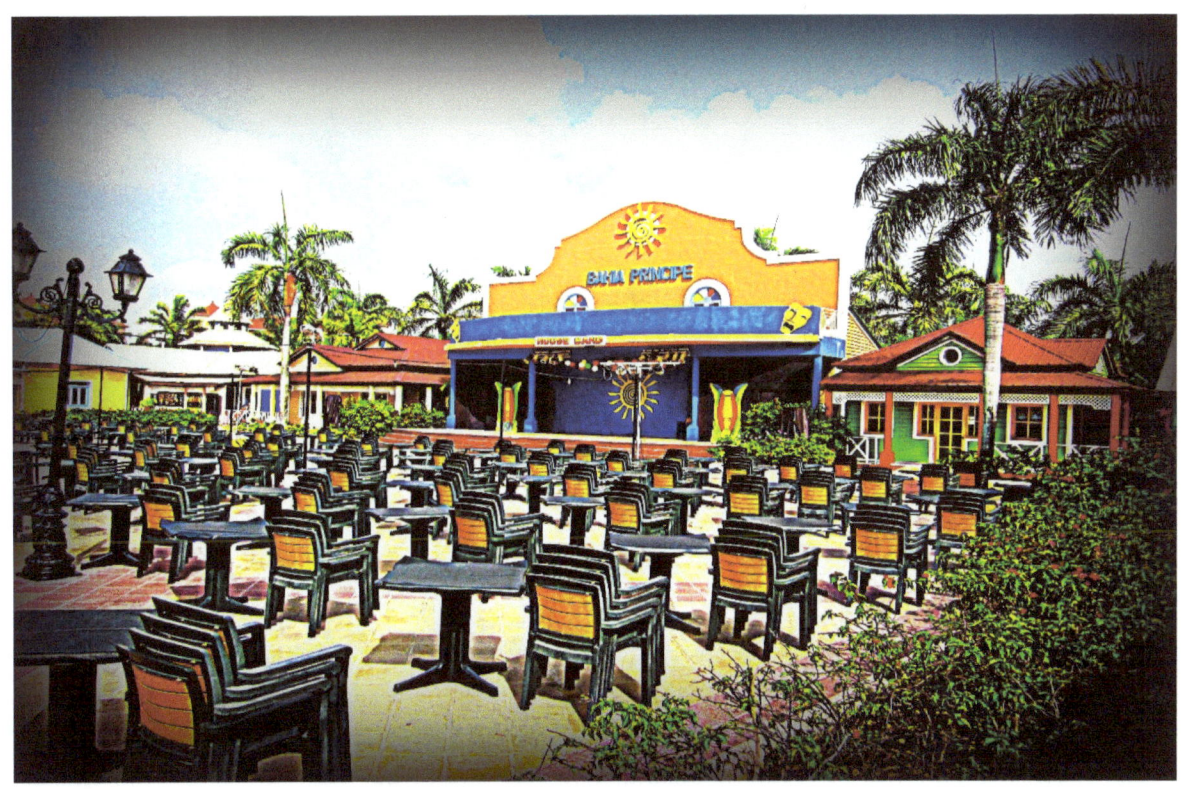

Bahia Principe

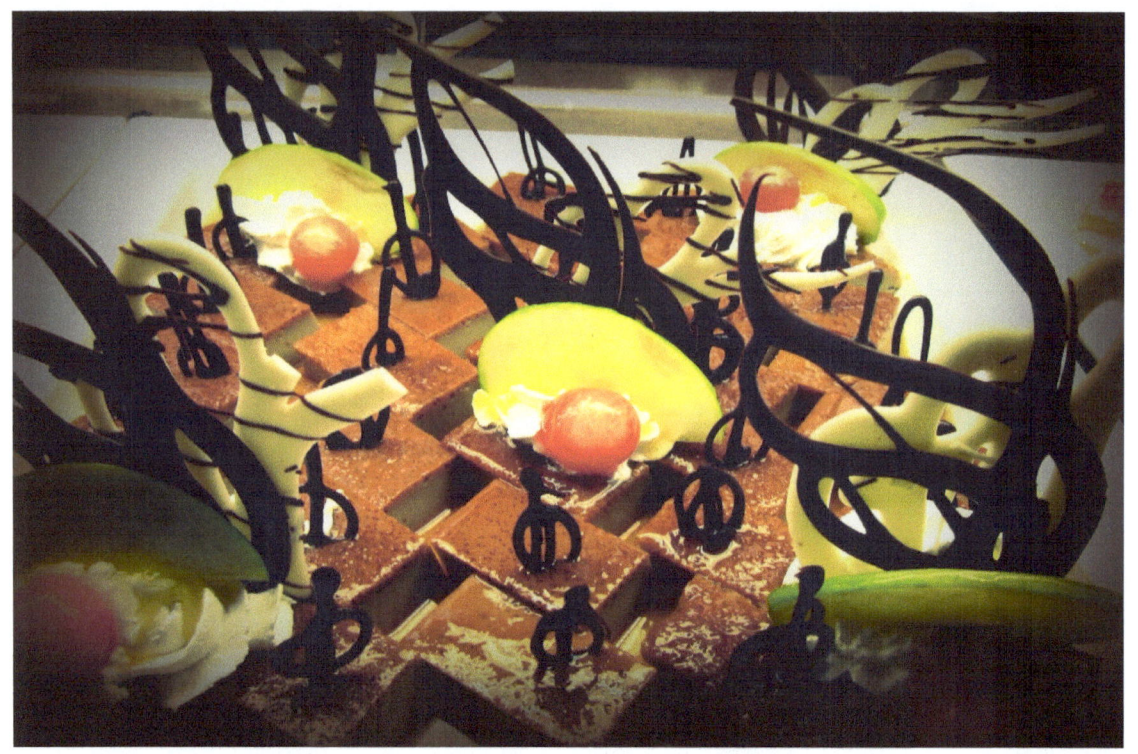

Just Desserts

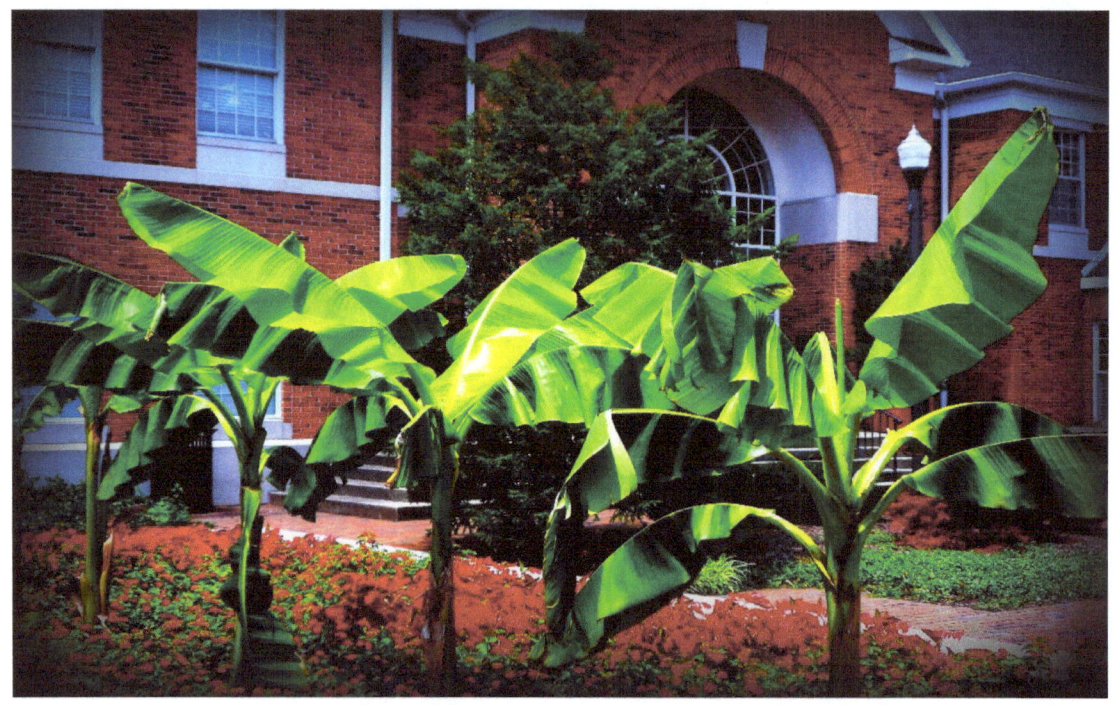

City Building Westerville, OH.

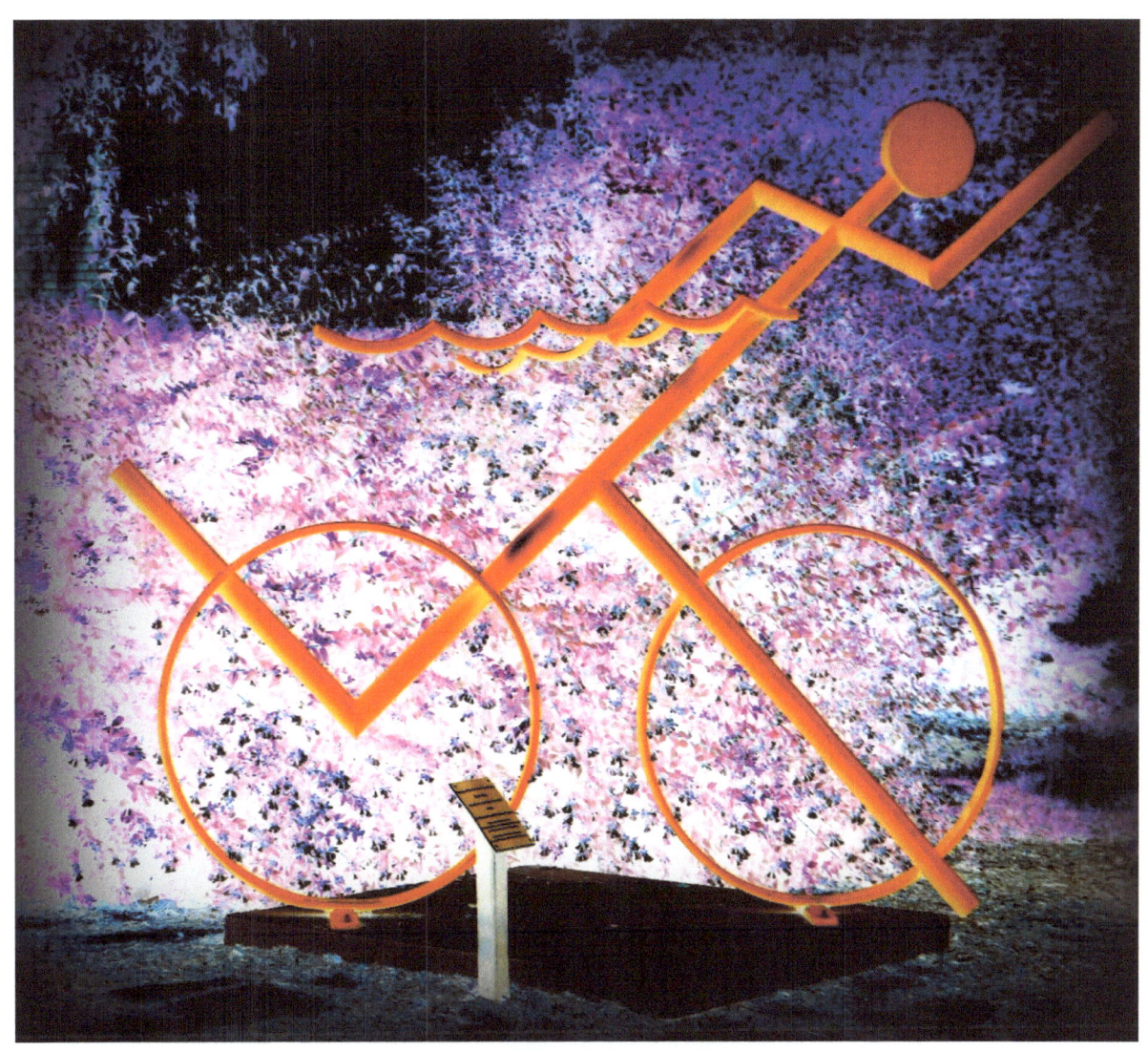

Westerville, OH

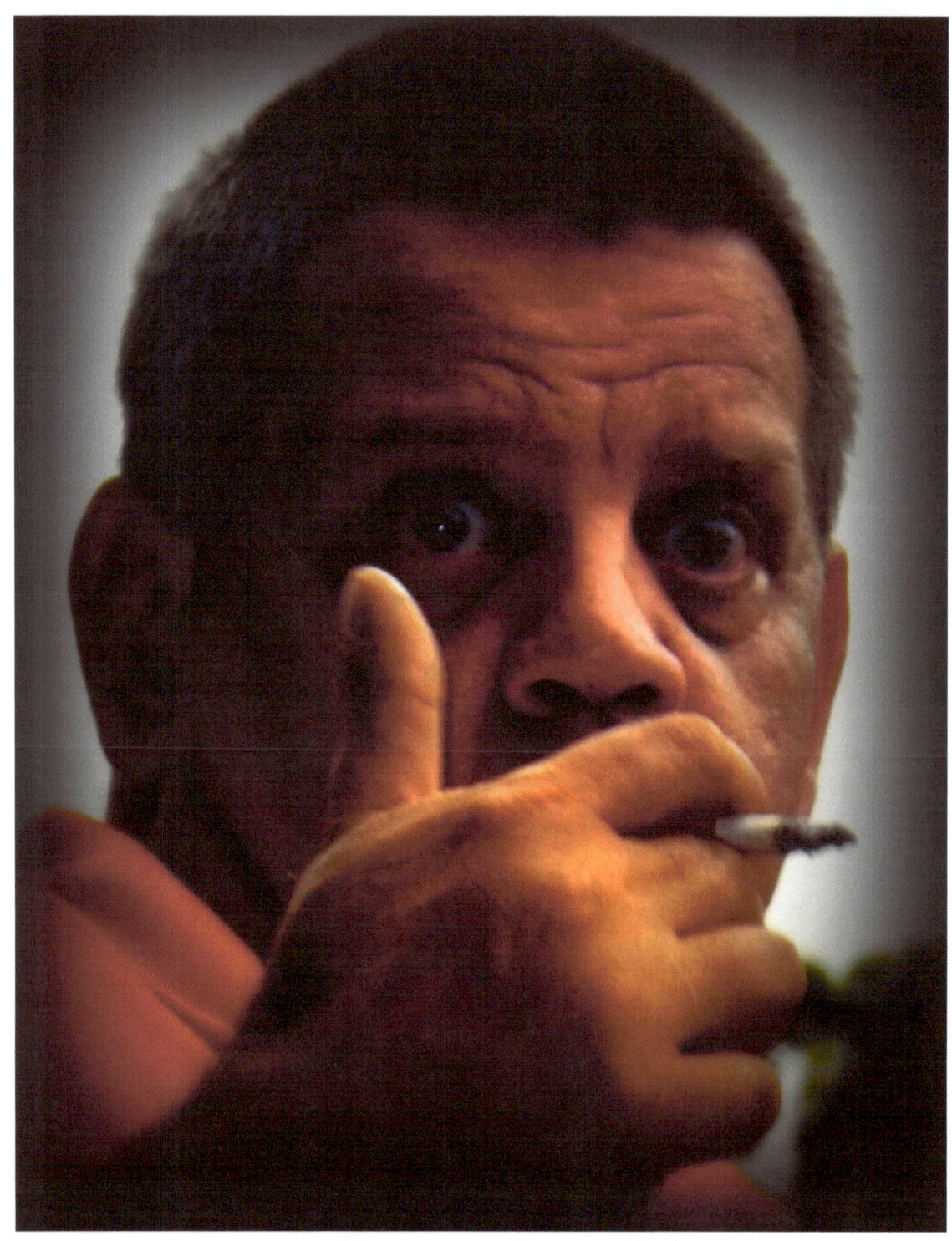

Dangerous Doug Price

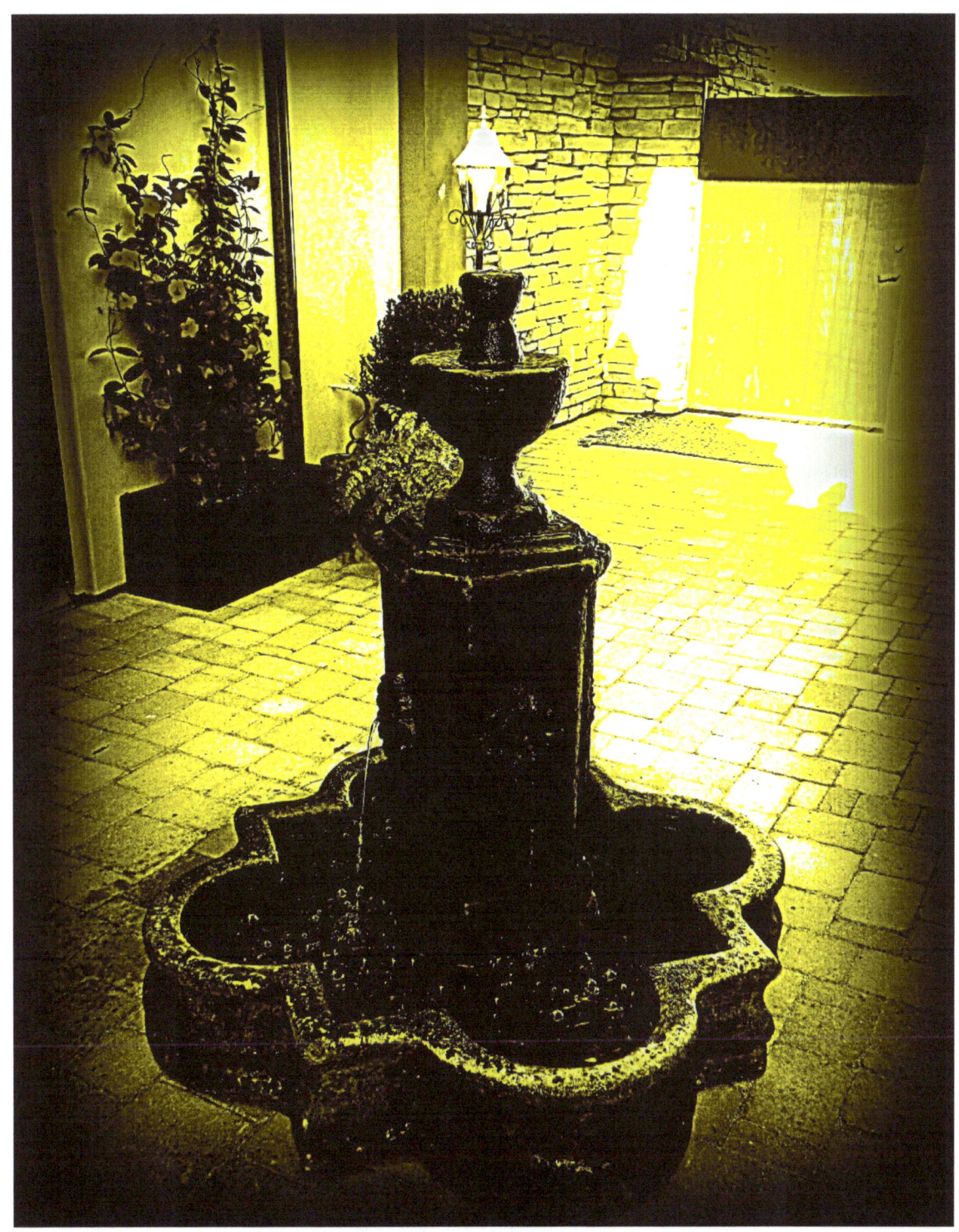

Barbara's Water Fountain

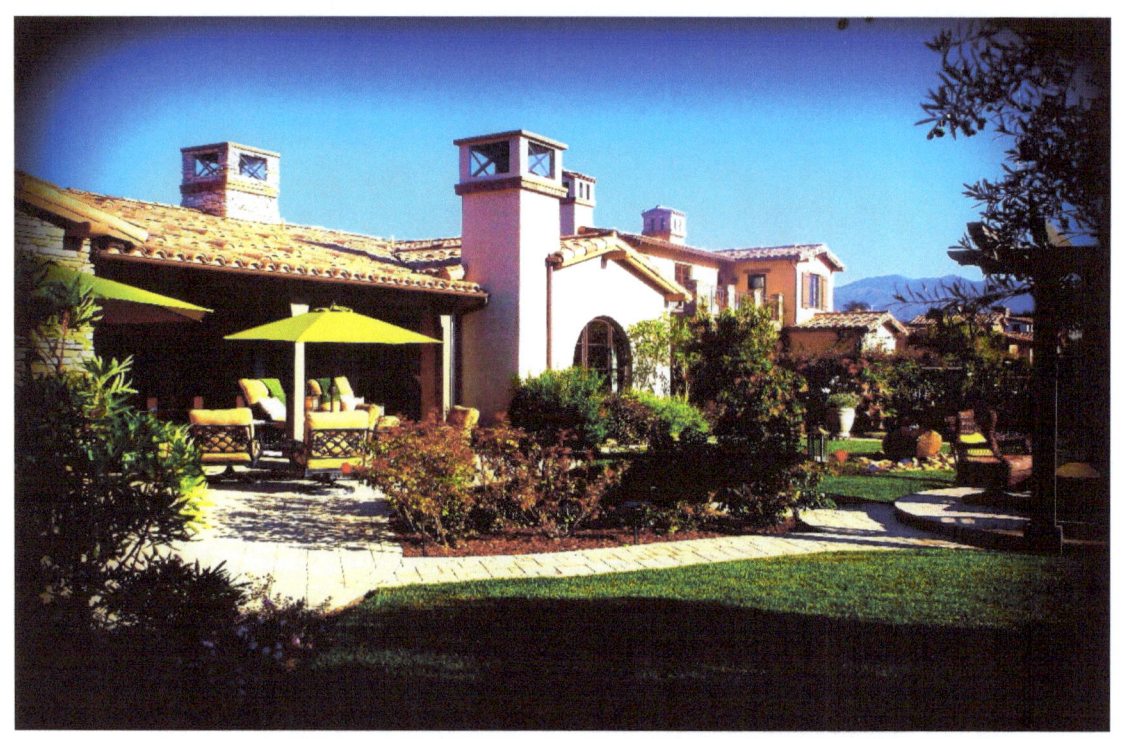

Marvelous Garden, California

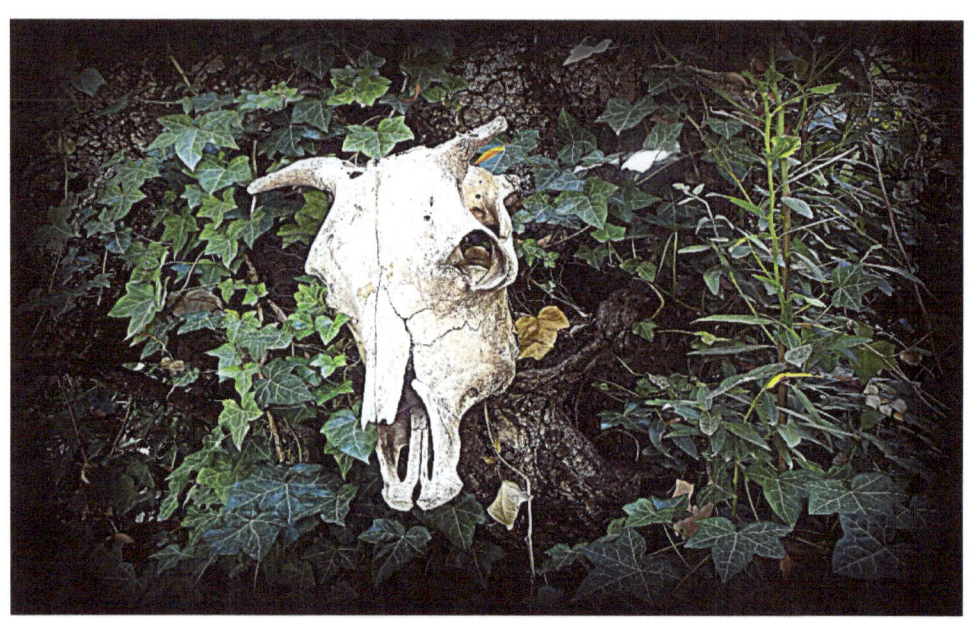

Head Case

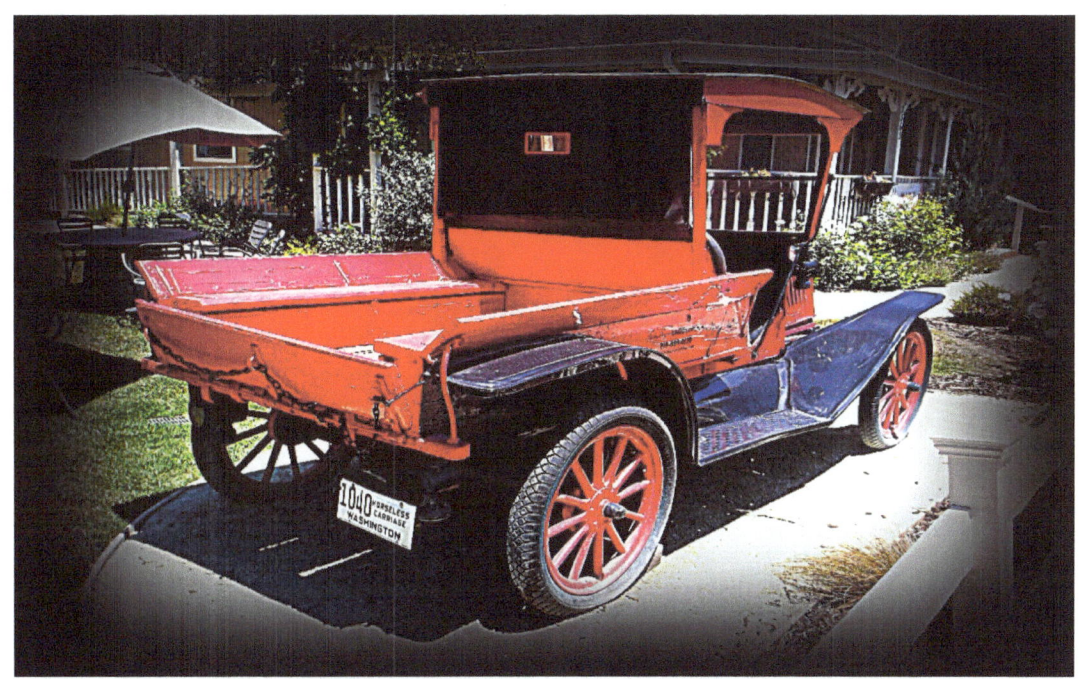

Santa Barbara, CA.

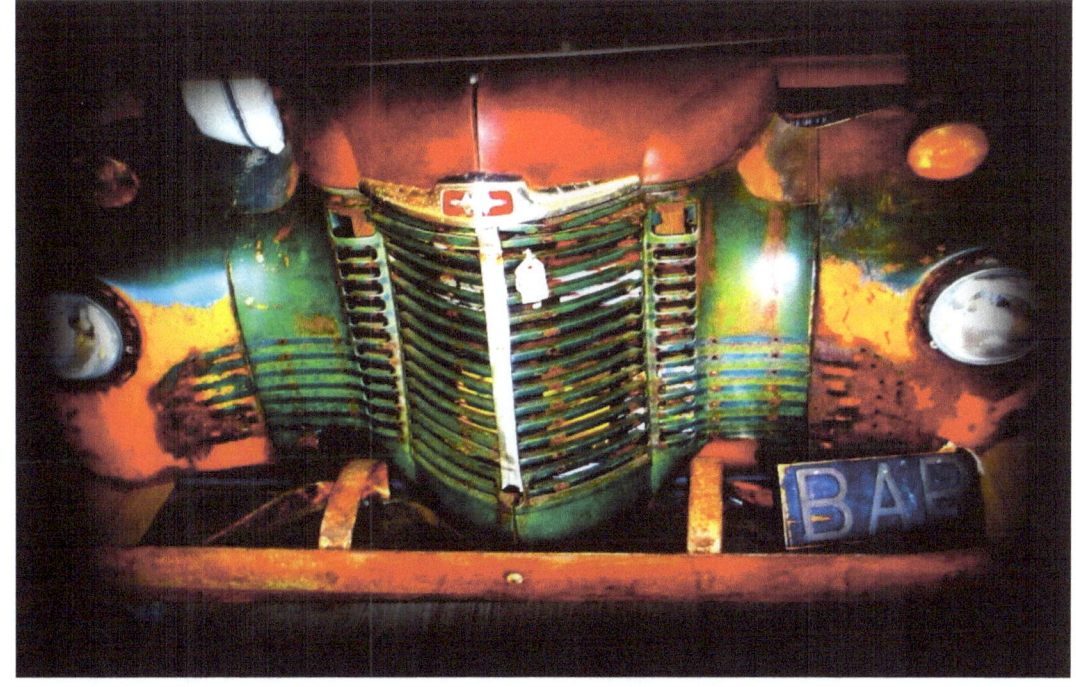

Californian Cocktail Bar

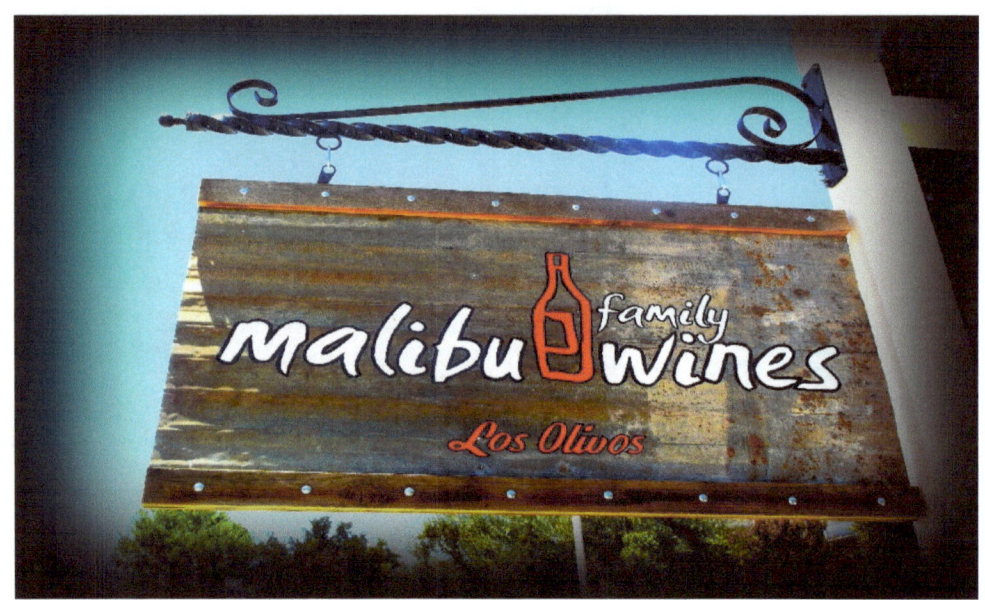

Malibu Watering Hole

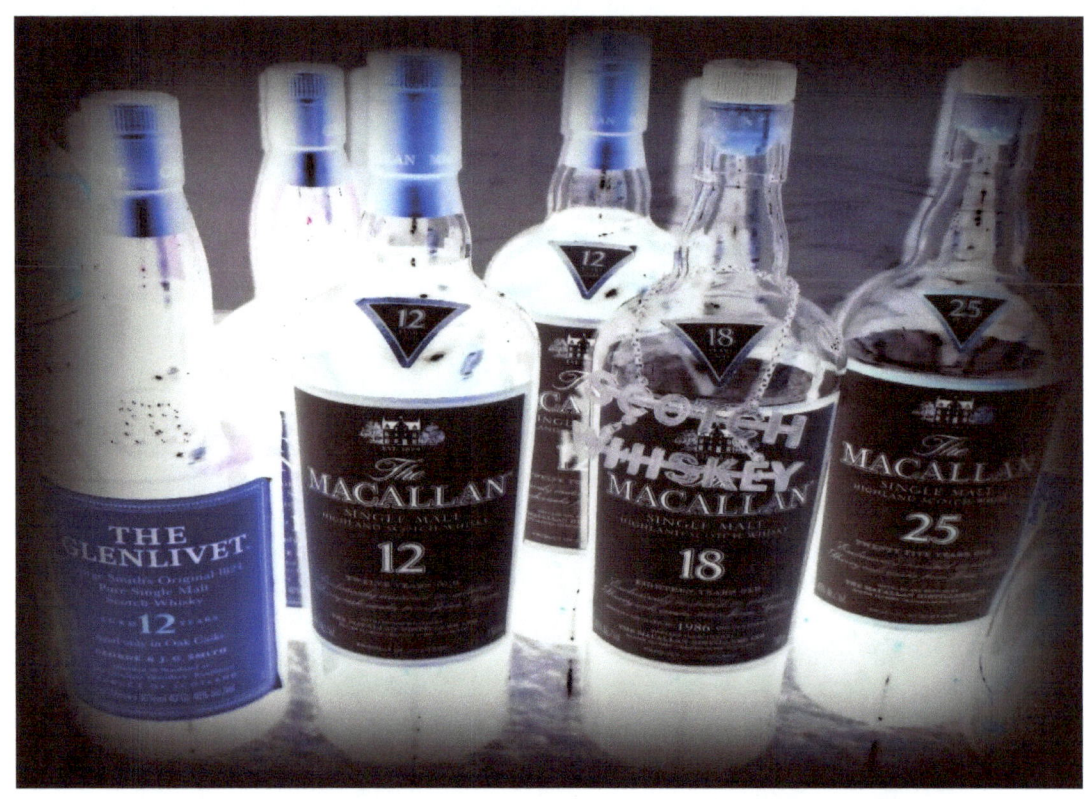

Highland Misty Fling

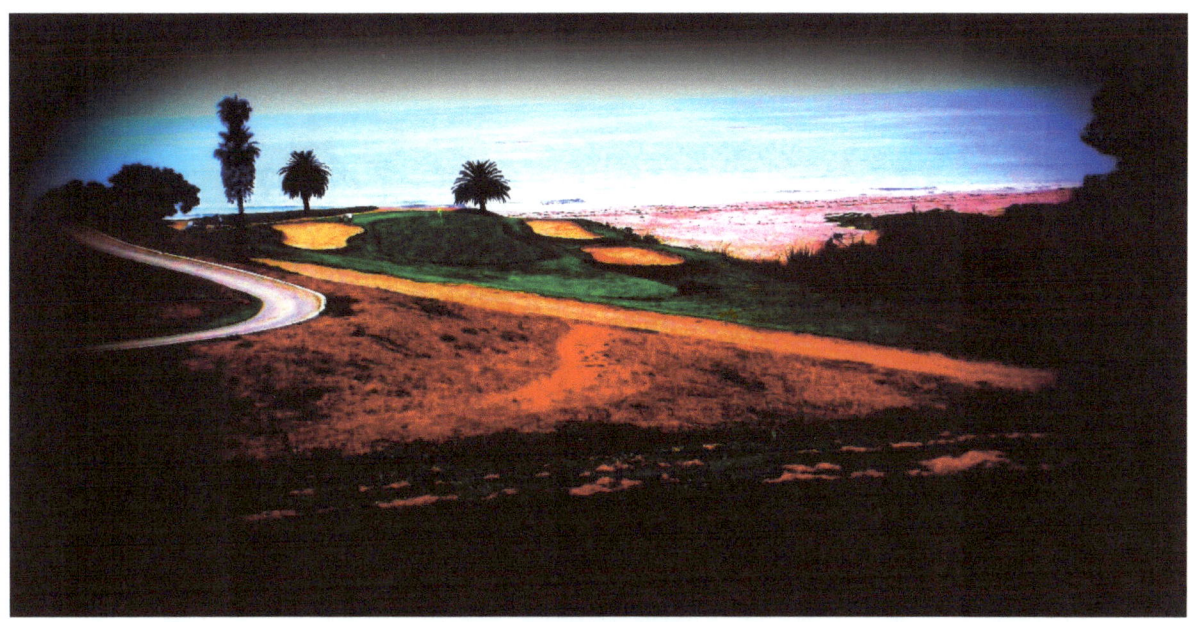

Californian Par Three

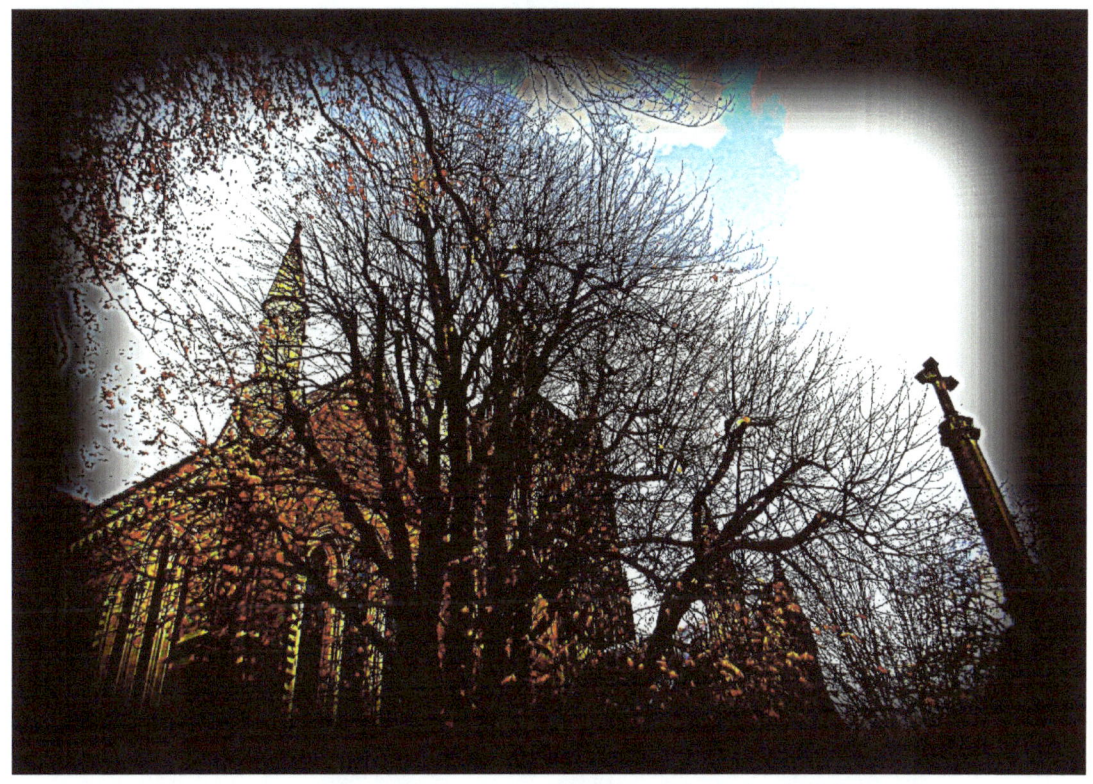

Worcester Cathedral UK

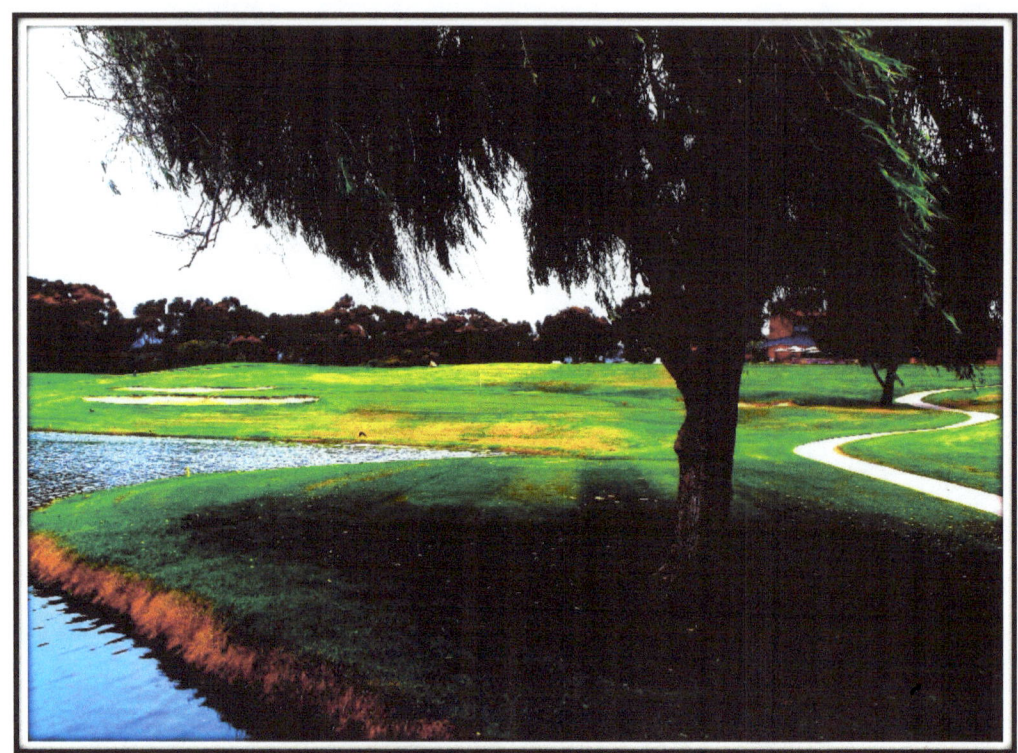

California Par Three II

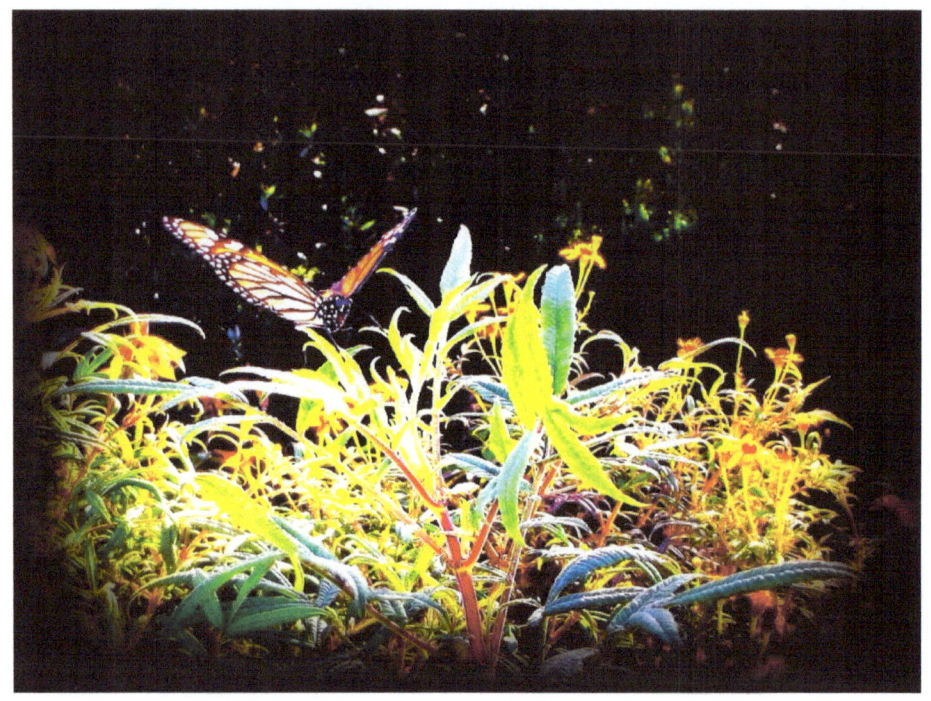

Santa Barbara Butterflyby

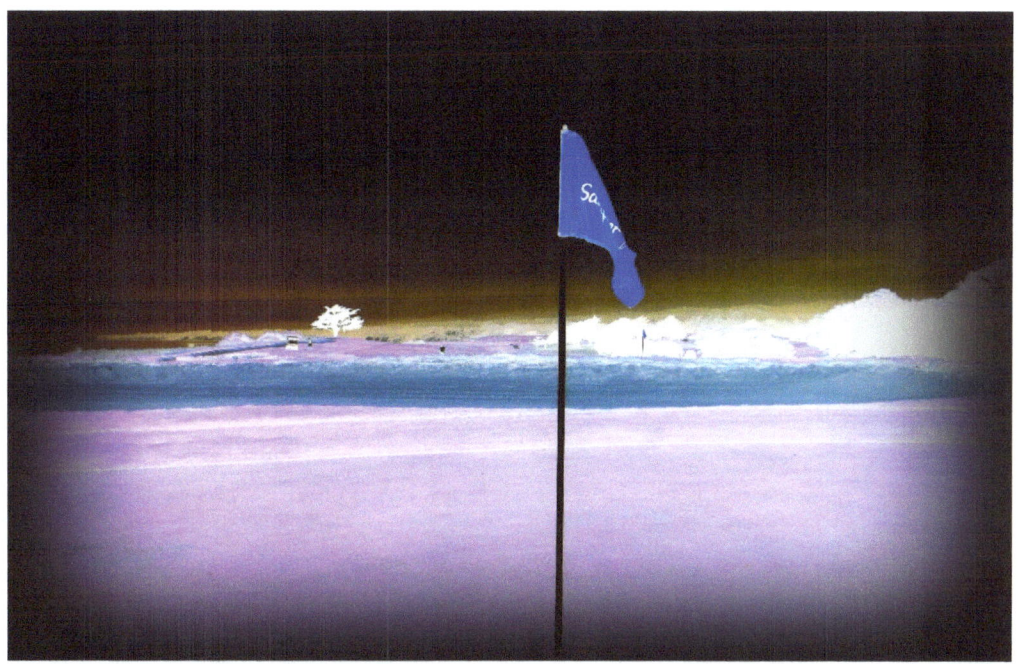

Santa Barbara Golf Club

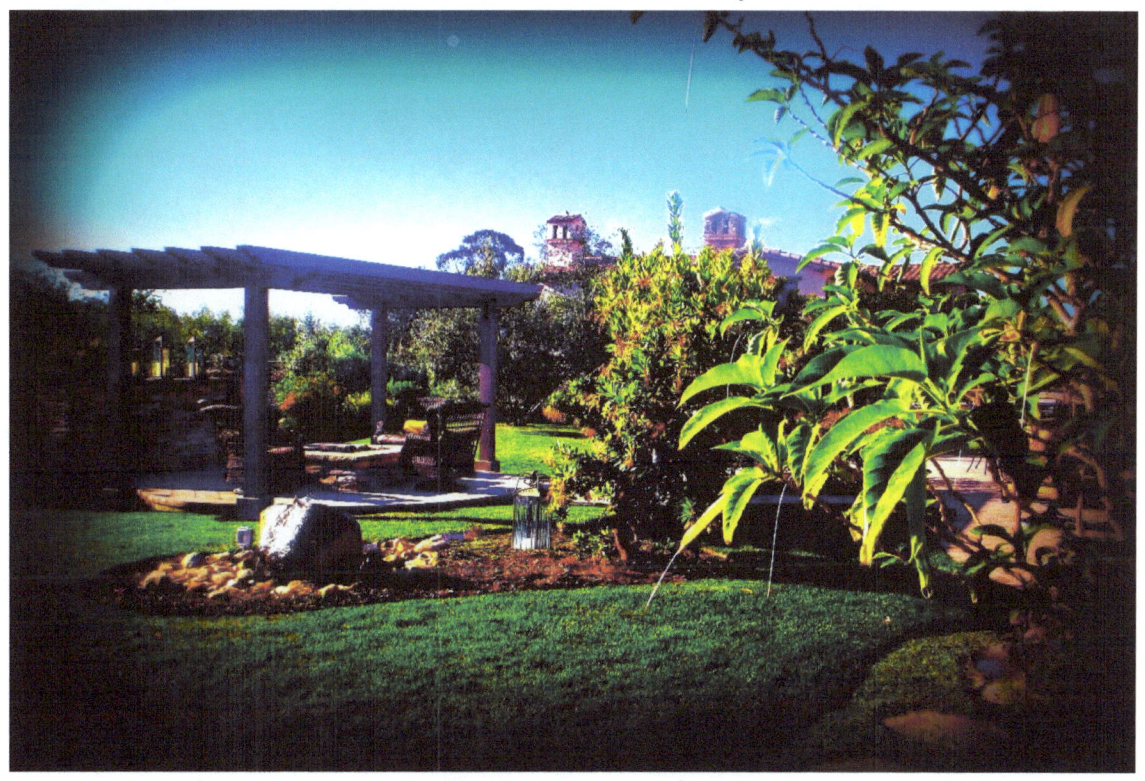

Brilliant Yard

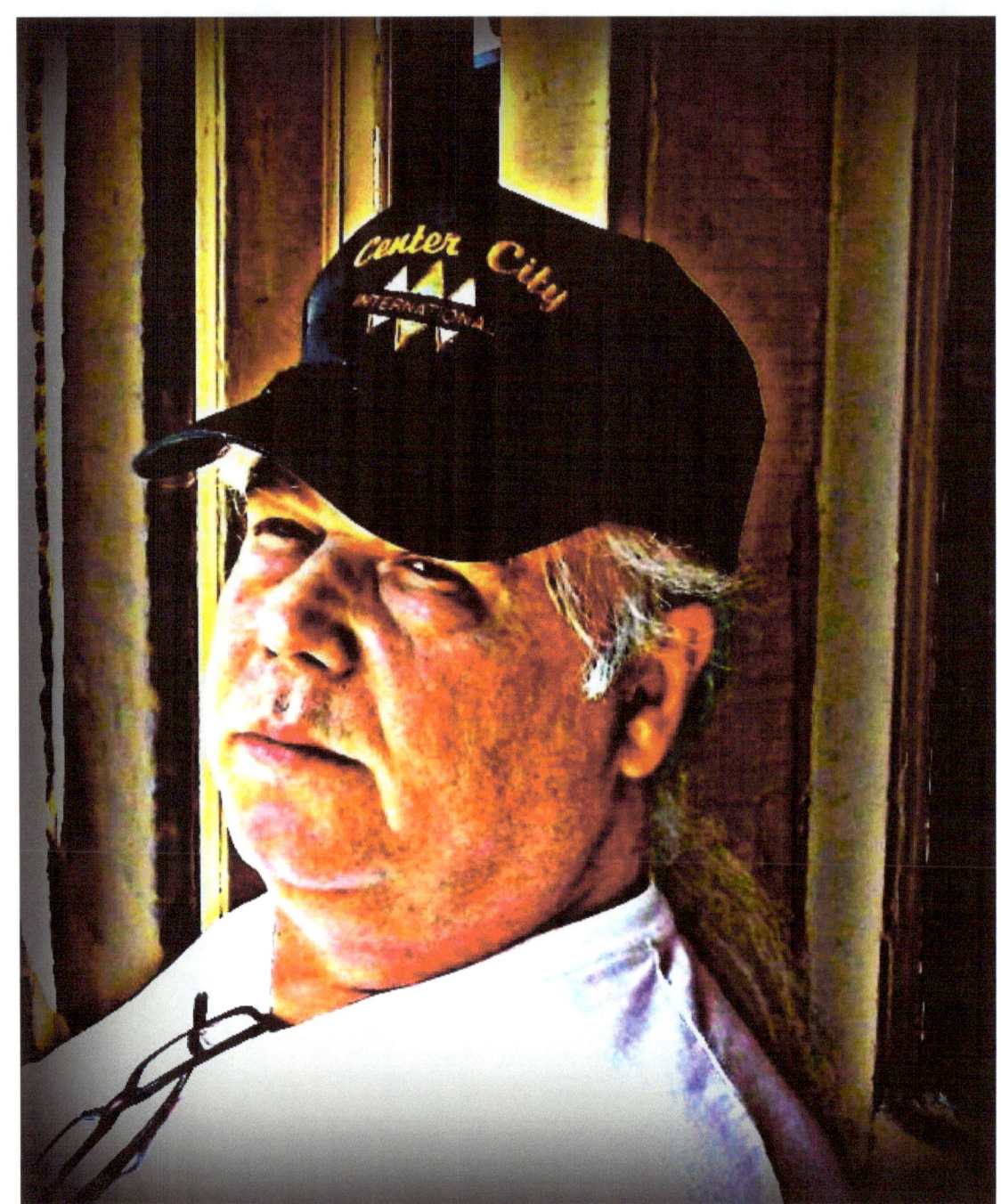

Dr. Shoe

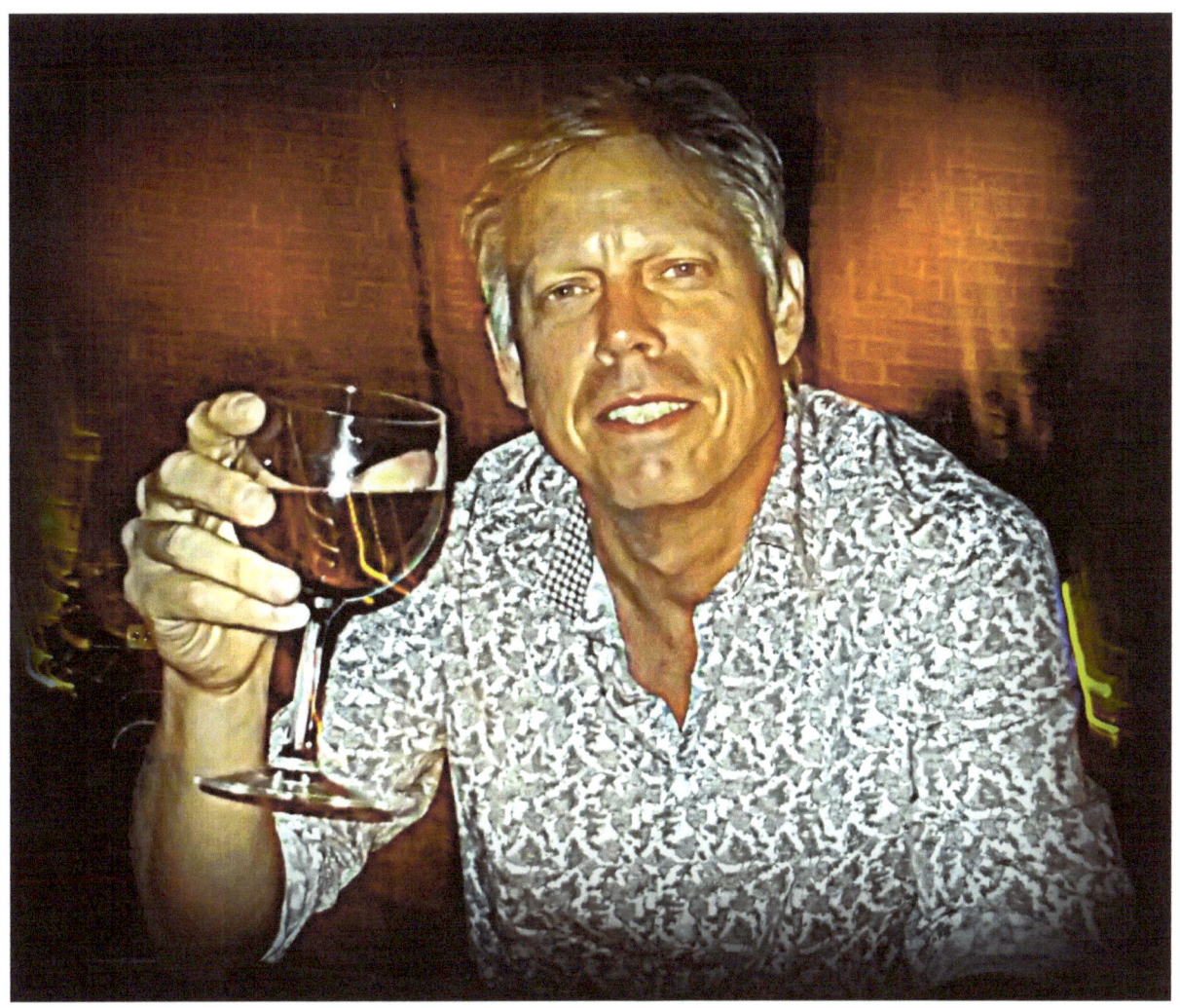

Tom Bowling and Friend – Cheer Mate

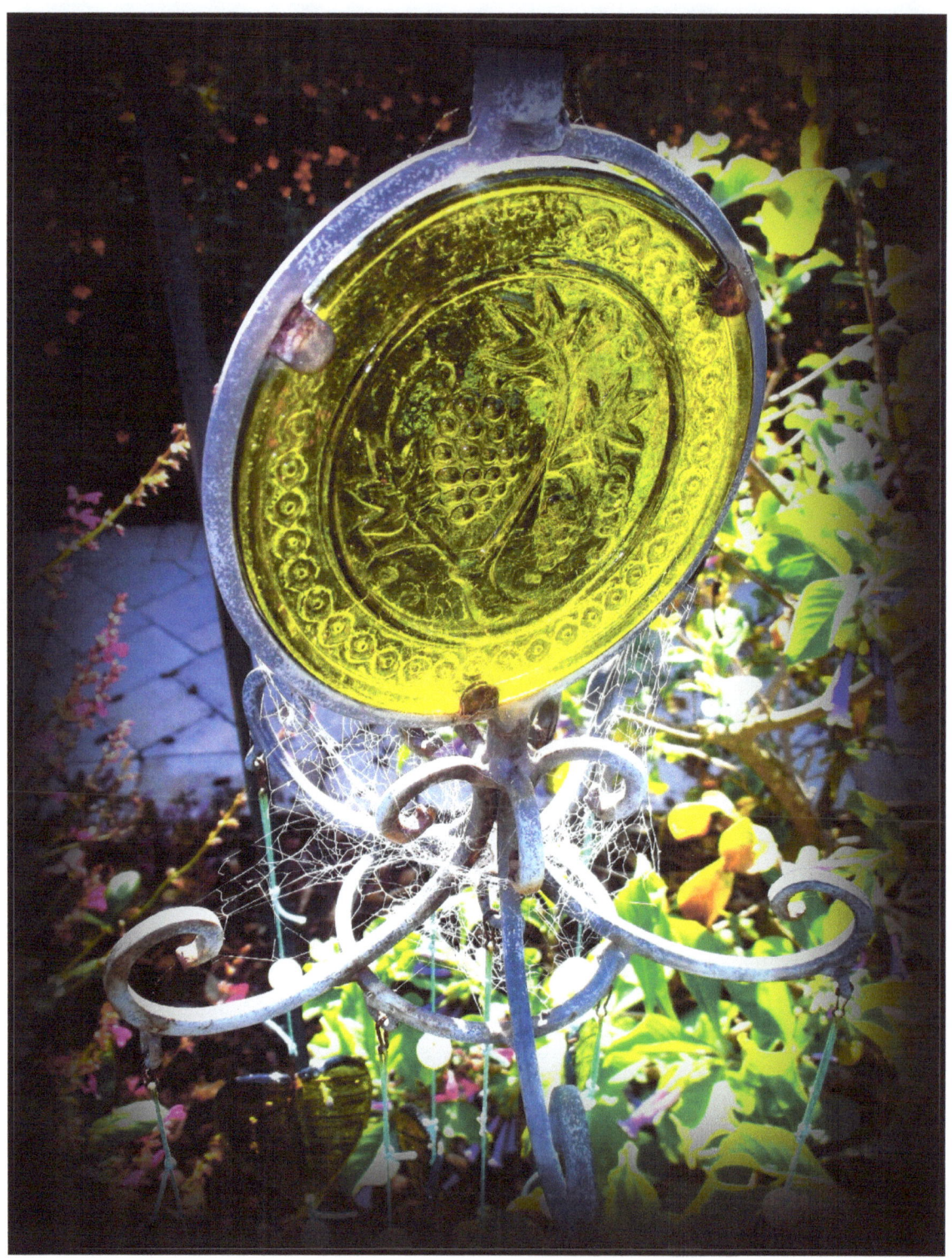

Glass and Cobwebs

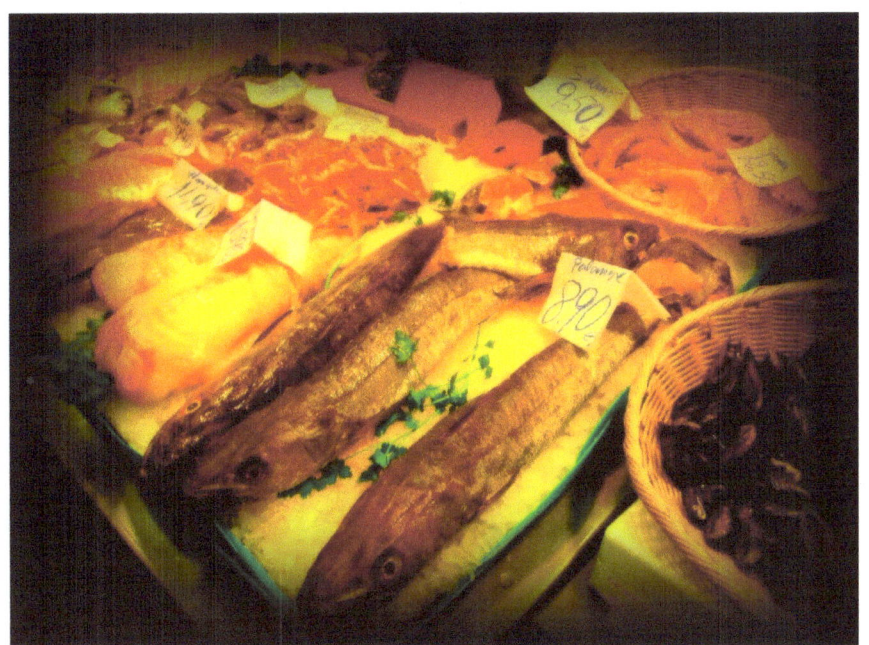

Fishy, Fish Fish

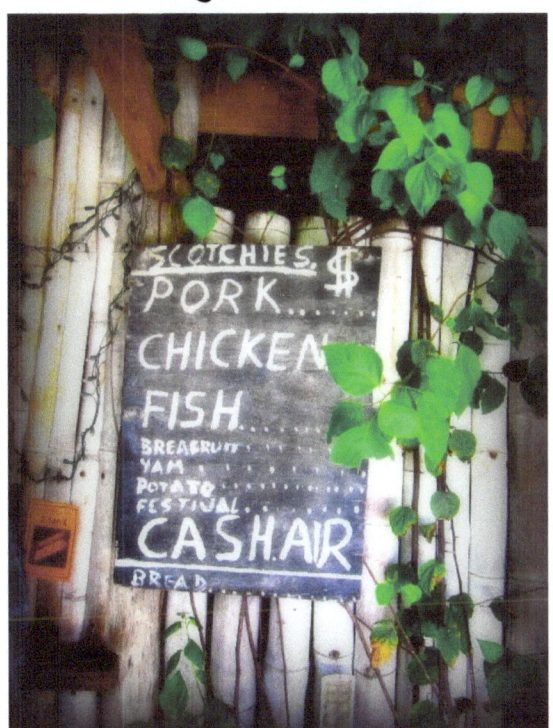

Perfect Menu Scotchie's Jamaica

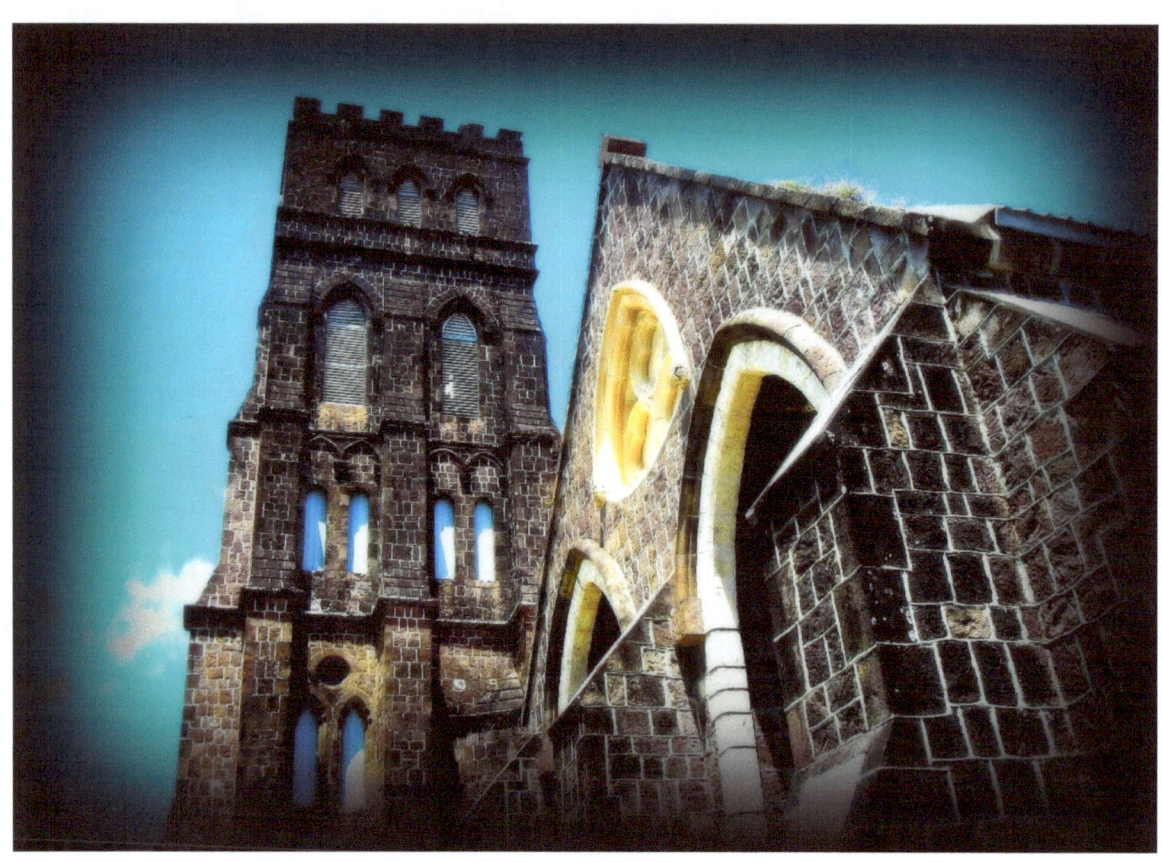

St. Thomas, Virgin Islands

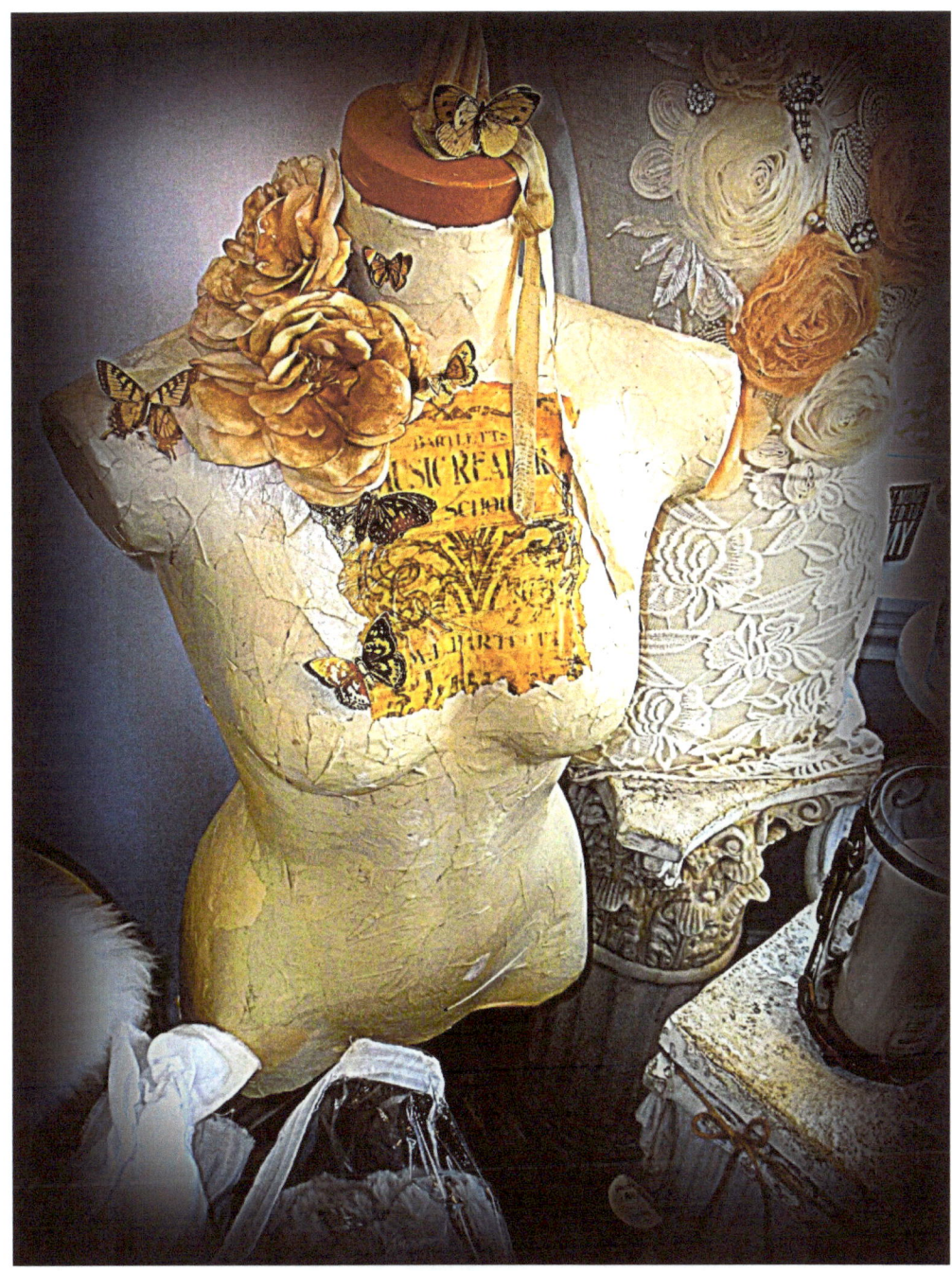

Are You Being Served?

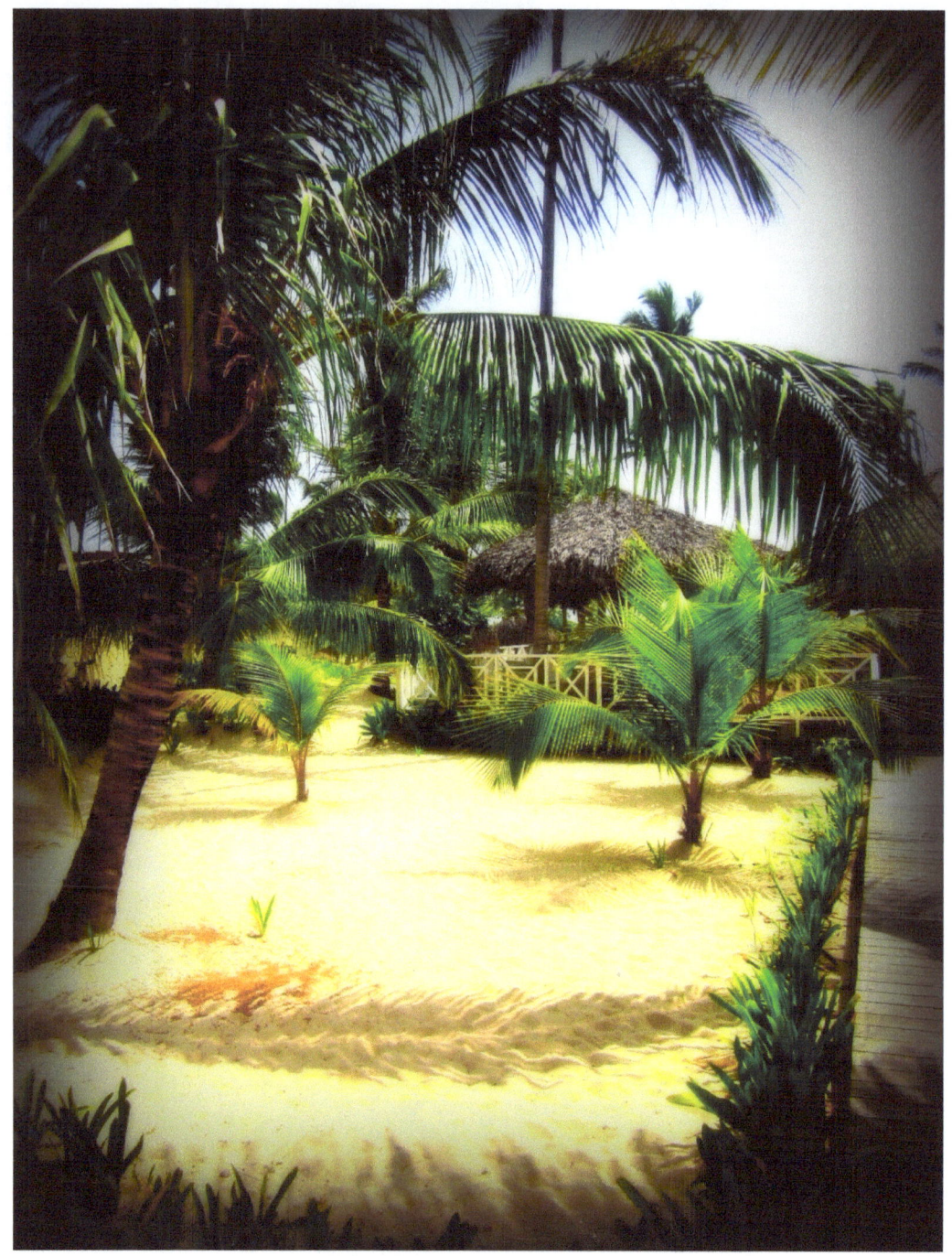

The End